Battleground Eu

The Defence
St Valery-en-Caux
1940

Also by Jerry Murland and published by Pen & Sword:

Aristocrats Go to War (2010)

Retreat and Rearguard 1914 (2011)

Battle on the Aisne 1914 (2012)

Battle Lines: Ypres – Nieuwpoort to Ploegsteert (with Jon Cooksey) (2012)

Aisne 1914 (2013)

Retreat of I Corps 1914 (2014)

Retreat and Rearguard Somme 1918 (2014)

The Retreat from Mons 1914: North (with Jon Cooksey) (2014)

The Retreat from Mons 1914: South (with Jon Cooksey) (2014)

The Battles of French Flanders: Neuve Chapelle, Aubers Ridge, Festubert, Loos and Fromelles (with Jon Cooksey) (2015)

The First Day of the Somme: Gommecourt to Maricourt (with Jon Cooksey) (2016)

Retreat and Rearguard Dunkirk 1940 (2016)

Battle for the Escaut 1940 (2016)

Cassel and Hazebrouck 1940 (2017)

Frankforce and the Defence of Arras 1940 (2017)

The Canal Line (2018)

The Battles of Arras: North (with Jon Cooksey) (2019)

The Battles of Arras: South (with Jon Cooksey) (2019)

The Dunkirk Perimeter and Evacuation 1940 (2019)

The Battle of the Ypres-Comines Canal 1940 (2019)

The Somme 1916 – Beyond the First Day: Beaucourt and Mametz Wood to the Butte de Warlencourt (with Jon Cooksey) (2021)

The Schneider Trophy Air Races (2021)

Allied Air Operations, 1939–1940 (2022)

The Battle of Cambrai 1917 (2022)

The Western Dunkirk Corridor 1940 (2022)

Battleground Europe

The Defence of St Valery-en-Caux 1940

The 51st (Highland) Division from The Saar to Normandy

Jerry Murland

Series Editor
Nigel Cave

Pen & Sword
MILITARY

First published in Great Britain in 2024 by
PEN & SWORD MILITARY
an imprint of Pen & Sword Books Ltd
Yorkshire – Philadelphia

ISBN 978-1-47385-227-3

Typeset by Concept, Huddersfield, West Yorkshire, HD4 5JL.
Printed and bound in England by CPI Group (UK) Ltd, Croydon CR0 4YY.

MIX
Paper | Supporting
responsible forestry
FSC
www.fsc.org FSC® C013604

Pen & Sword Books Ltd incorporates the imprints of Aviation, Atlas, Family History, Fiction, Maritime, Military, Discovery, Politics, History, Archaeology, Select, Wharncliffe Local History, Wharncliffe True Crime, Military Classics, Wharncliffe Transport, Leo Cooper, The Praetorian Press, Remember When, White Owl, Seaforth Publishing and Frontline Books.

For a complete list of Pen & Sword titles please contact
PEN & SWORD BOOKS LTD
47 Church Street, Barnsley, South Yorkshire, S70 2AS, England
E-mail: enquiries@pen-and-sword.co.uk
Website: www.pen-and-sword.co.uk
or
PEN & SWORD BOOKS
1950 Lawrence Rd, Havertown, PA 19083, USA
E-mail: uspen-and-sword@casematepublishers.com
Website: www.penandswordbooks.com

Contents

List of Maps

Introduction by the Series Editor

This is the last book in Jerry Murland's eight volume survey of the BEF's France and Flanders 1940 experience and which provides a comprehensive account (with tours) of its part in the devastating German offensive in the west. This campaign has been relegated in British popular culture to one event, that is the largely successful (albeit not concealing a disastrous military setback) evacuation from and around the Dunkirk beaches. This book largely, but not exclusively, concerns itself with the 51st (Highland) Division, in particular its defeat and surrender at St Valery-en-Caux; there were significant numbers of other BEF units involved, not to mention elements of the French Tenth Army, all of which receive due coverage.

In 1968, when I made my first visit to the battlefields, taken by my father from his posting in BAOR, and at the same age he was when his grandfather (7th Leicesters) took him in 1937, we were able to spend half an afternoon on a blazing hot August day on the Newfoundland Memorial site at Beaumont Hamel, having the place entirely to ourselves. When we came down to the Y Ravine area and the German trenches, I got my first close-up view of the magnificent Highland Division Memorial: its positioning and its execution were a work of genius.

It was then that my father told me about the fate of the 51st (Highland) Division in 1940, 'put into the bag' at St Valery. He also commented on the fact that the Division was particularly tasked with recapturing the seaside resort at the beginning of September 1944. It was undoubtedly the memorial at Beaumont Hamel that triggered his memory; but looking back at it I find it interesting that he recalled the story so well. I must admit that it took me some years to realise that the St Valery in question was not the one at the mouth of the Somme but a fairly short distance further south down the Atlantic coast, in the Seine-Maritime Département.

It is not altogether unsurprising, given the circumstances surrounding the outbreak of the Second World War, that the Division was rather less 'Highland' and Territorial in composition than its predecessor in the previous war, which managed to remain almost entirely Scottish – and Highland – for the duration. Some of the units were able to survive the disaster at St Valery (notably those of 154 Brigade) to some degree and it was a notable tribute that the Division was reformed in the UK in August 1940, admittedly by the simple expedient of renaming the 9th (Highland) Division – which in the Great War had been simply 'Scottish' – as the 51st.

This book is the story of an underprepared Division being shipped out to France in January 1940 before it was fully trained; in due course it was transferred to the Saar Front under French command, entering the line in early May. The Division never served in the line with the main body of the BEF under Lord Gort. Like so many BEF formations, it endured a bewildering series of events that commenced in the Saar, saw them transported across France and then coming under the command of the French Tenth Army in the western Somme area. Within a matter of weeks from first contact with the enemy the war was over for the bulk of the members of the Division, along with others who had been despatched to the Somme front whilst the main evacuation was taking place to the north. Although the surrender at St Valery on 12 June was not strictly the end of the BEF's time in France in 1940 – there were major evacuations from Havre, Brest, Cherbourg and St Malo, Nantes and St Nazaire, amongst others – it did mark the end of the army's active involvement.

The French applied for an armistice on 17 June. The French government then announced, on 24 June, that all evacuations must cease on the 25th as part of the armistice terms with the Germans. In fact, evacuations continued, notably from French Mediterranean ports, until 14 August. On top of the many thousands evacuated under Operation Dynamo, over half as many again, some 192,000, were evacuated from ports and beaches south of the Somme. Doubtless the events in western Europe were a military catastrophe for the allies; but it could have been worse and the generally successful evacuation of so many allied troops – minus all their heavy equipment, it has to be said – was notable. Although often downplayed, not without reason, as a triumph of myth and propaganda over reality, the evacuation from the beaches and the ports of northern and western France achieved more than a 'feel-better' story. One must consider what the consequence would have been if the Germans had managed to capture the great bulk of the men who were evacuated. What would the impact have been on the willingness and capability to continue fighting, not only of the British but also on the establishment of significant Free French and Polish forces abroad?

The allied cause suffered a massive blow in 1940. It – and its consequences – were so uncomfortable that France has never commissioned an official history of the Second World War, a stark contrast to the more than 100 volumes that cover its effort in the First World War. Its consequence was the end of any resistance to the German will (except that organised from governments in exile and by a very limited number of necessarily often *ad hoc* and disorganised resistance groups) in most of continental Europe.

*   *   *

Currently (2024) in eastern Europe, in Ukraine, thousands of young men – mainly – have been sent into the field and many of them have become casualties, all in a matter of two years. Civilian casualties have been very high, and the destruction of towns, villages and infrastructure has been enormous. Thus, what was unimaginable a few years ago – a major European war – is now being played out before our eyes and with no end in sight. Working as I do on various aspects of the two world wars, I have been struck by what a dramatic effect war has had – and will continue to have – on those who have been drafted into serving in the forces.

When war broke out in 1914, my then twenty-one year old grandfather was working in the accounts department of a wholesale textile firm in Leicester, having broken from a family tradition of working in the railways (his illiterate great grandfather was killed shunting trains in Leicester). At the time he was learning Spanish, with a view to emigrating to Argentina, a boom economy in the early twentieth century. He enlisted in the Leicesters in September 1914 and survived the war more or less unscathed. After hostilities ended he stayed in the army, served in the Western Desert in the Second World War and ended his military career a couple of years after its end as a major, the QM of the Leicesters' Depot in Glen Parva. His life had been completely transformed by a war that he survived unscathed.

My father, then sixteen years old, was at school at Stonyhurst College at the outbreak of the Second World War. He obtained a place to go to St Andrews to read Greats, the first member of the branch of the Cave family to achieve this leap into higher education. However, as soon as he left school he opted to join the army and served in India, Italy and Greece. Like my grandfather, at the end of hostilities he decided to stay in the army, making it his career, retiring in 1974 as a colonel and Defence Attaché in Prague. He, too, came through the war unscathed; he, too, had his life completely redirected by conflict. In both cases they would never have met their future wives if they had not served in the military.

The point of this, perhaps indulgent, digression from St Valery is to consider how war can change lives so much. There are the obvious consequences of sudden, young death or grievous long-term wounds, physical and mental; there is material destruction; there is massive civil and economic dislocation during the wartime years and in the immediate aftermath; civilian casualties have grown ever larger and more indiscriminate as warfare has developed through the twentieth century and beyond. I am sure that we who come afterwards all consider these traumatic effects; but it has also struck me recently – probably prompted by the events in Ukraine – how many lives were directed into completely unexpected paths by war. So when I consider the men described in this series of books (and they were nearly all men) I have thought far more of the long term impact of war on those who were not medical or fatal casualties, how its effect was, is and undoubtedly will continue to be, so far reaching and so unpredictable in the lives of each and every person involved in it.

Nigel Cave
Ratcliffe College, February 2024

Author's Introduction

The story of the 51st (Highland) Division during 1939 and 1940 is a short and largely tragic one and, although it burnt itself into the minds of Scotsmen, it has never been granted the recognition it deserves. Even in Scotland it was often forgotten that the men, and attached troops, of the 51st Division, were fighting for survival in Normandy for some ten days *after* the evacuation from Dunkerque had been completed. Most present-day accounts of the Second World War in 1939/40 deal with the 'Phoney War' and the evacuation from Dunkerque; few mention the rear-guard action at St Valery-en-Caux other than giving it a passing mention. Nevertheless, the action of the 51st Division against the might of the German forces won the admiration of General Erwin Rommel and Charles de Gaulle, who fought alongside them. De Gaulle is on record about his admiration for the Highlanders:

> The valiant 51st (Highland) Division, under General Fortune, played its part in the decision which I took to continue fighting on the side of the Allies unto the end no matter what may be the course of events.

One of the enduring beliefs of the war is that Churchill deliberately sacrificed the 51st Division in an attempt to keep France in the war. This, apart from being palpably incorrect, fails miserably to address the intricacy of the circumstances that overtook the 51st Division after they returned from the Saar. It was a situation where units were repeatedly changing affiliation, where communication between the French Supreme Command and British forces suffered from a lack of fluency with each other's language and the inclination to blame one another for the debacle that inevitably ensued. Nevertheless, for all the criticism that is thrown at the French Army, it is clear that a number of French units fought hard and with great courage, the main fault with the French command lying with poor leadership and lack of tactical planning.

So far as the Highlanders were concerned it was bad luck that their tour of duty on the Saar coincided with the beginning of *Fall Rot*. The speed and extent of the German advance from Abbeville took their own High Command and the French by surprise and it was with little wonder that Allied military thinking failed to keep up with actions on the battlefield. The theory that Churchill sacrificed the Division to keep the French in the war owes a great deal to the need to attribute all the misery of the world to one scoundrel, a Scottish trait that some might say exists to this day! The sacrifice theory seems an easy one to support; but Churchill's liability appears to be confined mainly to one written account; even Sir Derek Lang, the Adjutant of the 4/Cameron Highlanders at the time and a subsequent escaper, disagreed with this naive description of events. Churchill himself recorded his personal grief at the loss of the 51st Division in his *Their Finest Hour: The Second World War*, Volume 2.

Churchill was not to know that Britain could survive a French capitulation nor that the Battle of Britain could be won and that, thanks to the RAF and Royal Navy, there would be no invasion. Unfortunately, after Dunkirk, the assistance offered to the troops south of the Somme was negligible and any deployment of aircraft necessarily involved the RAF from English bases rather than those that were based in France.

It is true that Churchill's support of France was far reaching and that was, to an extent, underlined by the despatch of Sir Alan Brooke, who was ordered to return to France to form a second BEF. The 52nd (Lowland) Division landed in France on the very day that the 51st Division was called upon to surrender. Brooke, as the Commander-in-Chief of British Forces in France, recommended that all British troops should be evacuated to England and over 50,000 men were evacuated from St Malo, Cherbourg and Le Havre. Evacuation of British troops continued from Nantes, St Nazaire and Bordeaux and a grand total of 144,000 British and 48,000 French and associated troops had been rescued in addition to the numbers evacuated from the beaches and port of Dunkerque. When the 51st Division surrendered at St Valery-en-Caux it was as if Scotland had surrendered itself and the lives of so many men were curtailed and imprisoned for the duration of the war.

Readers of this volume will notice that I have not included many of the decorations and awards made to individuals unless there is an occasion that demands it. In a number of cases the story of the 51st Division has been shortened considerably, which is simply to do with space. It would be impossible to include accounts of all the fighting as well as tell the story of how the 51st Division ended its days at St Valery-en-Caux. All information is correct at the time of writing.

Ranks and Abbreviations

PSM is an abbreviation of Platoon Sergeant Major, an appointment that was short lived and carried the rank of warrant officer class III (WO III). Armoured regiments, such as the 1/Lothian and Border Horse Yeomanry, used the rank of Troop Sergeant Major (TSM). Created in 1938, no promotions to the rank were given after 1940 and the rank disappeared.

The ranks given to each individual were those held in 1939–40 and do not represent subsequent promotion received, unless stated. When describing the fighting I have often referred to modern day road numbering in order to give the reader using current maps a more precise location.

When describing units and formations I have used a form of abbreviation, for example, the 1st Lothian and Border Yeomanry becomes the

1/Lothians and the 2nd Battalion Seaforth Highlanders becomes 2/Seaforths. Similarly the 51st (Highland) Division becomes the 51st Division.

German units and formations are largely similar to the British and all I have done with these is to shorten the words Infantry Regiment to IR, thus IR 25 is Infantry Regiment 25. Each infantry battalion was broken down into companies, each of whom is given an Arabic numeral, for example 3 Kompany.

Below is a list of equivalent ranks which may go some way to assisting the reader understanding the correlation between British, French and German ranks:

British	French	German
Field Marshal	Maréchal de France	Generalfeldmarschall
General	Géneral d'Armée	Generaloberst
Lieutenant-General	Général de Corps	General der Infantrie
Major General	Général de Division	Generalmajor
Brigadier	Général de Brigade	–
Colonel	Colonel	Oberst
Lieutenant Colonel	Lieutenant Colonel	Oberstleutnant
Major	Commandant/Major	Major
Captain	Capitaine	Hauptmann
Lieutenant	Lieutenant	Oberleutnant
Second Lieutenant	Sous-Lieutenant	Leutnant
Warrant Officer	Adjutant	Feldwebelleutnant
Sergeant Major	Sergeant Major	Offizierstellverteter
Sergeant	Sergeant	Vize Feldwebel
Corporal	Caporal	Unteroffizer
Lance Corporal	–	Gefreiter
Private	Soldat, Chasseur	Jaeger, Schütze

Early History

St Valery-en-Caux is a small fishing port and light industrial town situated in the Pays de Caux, some 20 miles (32 km) west of Dieppe, at the junction of the D53, D20, D79 and the D925 roads. Here huge chalk cliffs rise up from the pebble beach to overlook the English Channel. The SNCF railway station was closed in the 1990s; on 17 January 1945, the railway station was destroyed when a runaway train carrying American troops crashed into it. A total of 89 American soldiers were killed and 152 injured. The only public transport now available is an infrequent bus service.

The town is said to have been founded by Saint Valery in the seventh century. A monastery was built on the site of the present-day town and was known as 'Sanctum Walaricum' (according to the charter in which Richard I, Duke of Normandy, gave the town to the Abbey of Fécamp). St Valery-en-Caux was a busy fishing port between the thirteenth and seventeenth centuries, its decline due to the growth of the much larger port of Fécamp, to the west.

The town was partly destroyed in the fighting involving the Germans and the 51st (Highland) Division in 1940. It has a casino and water park and has achieved the highest rating of four flowers in the annual 'France in Bloom' competition. Tourism now accounts for much of the town's prosperity. St Valery-en-Caux is the most recent town to be twinned with Inverness. This twinning had its roots in the historic ties between the two towns, which have been in place since the Second World War. Initial links between Inverness and St Valery were created when the 51st (Highland) Division were captured there in 1940 by the Germans. It is also twinned with Sontheim in southern Germany. The local people were very kind to the troops and the favour was returned when the Division returned in 1944, led by Lieutenant Colonel Derek Lang, to liberate the town. More than 70 per cent of St Valery was destroyed in the war and a special fund was set up in Inverness in order to send aid to the stricken town in a gesture of continuing fellowship. There have been many visits over the years between

A modern map of St Valery-en-Caux.

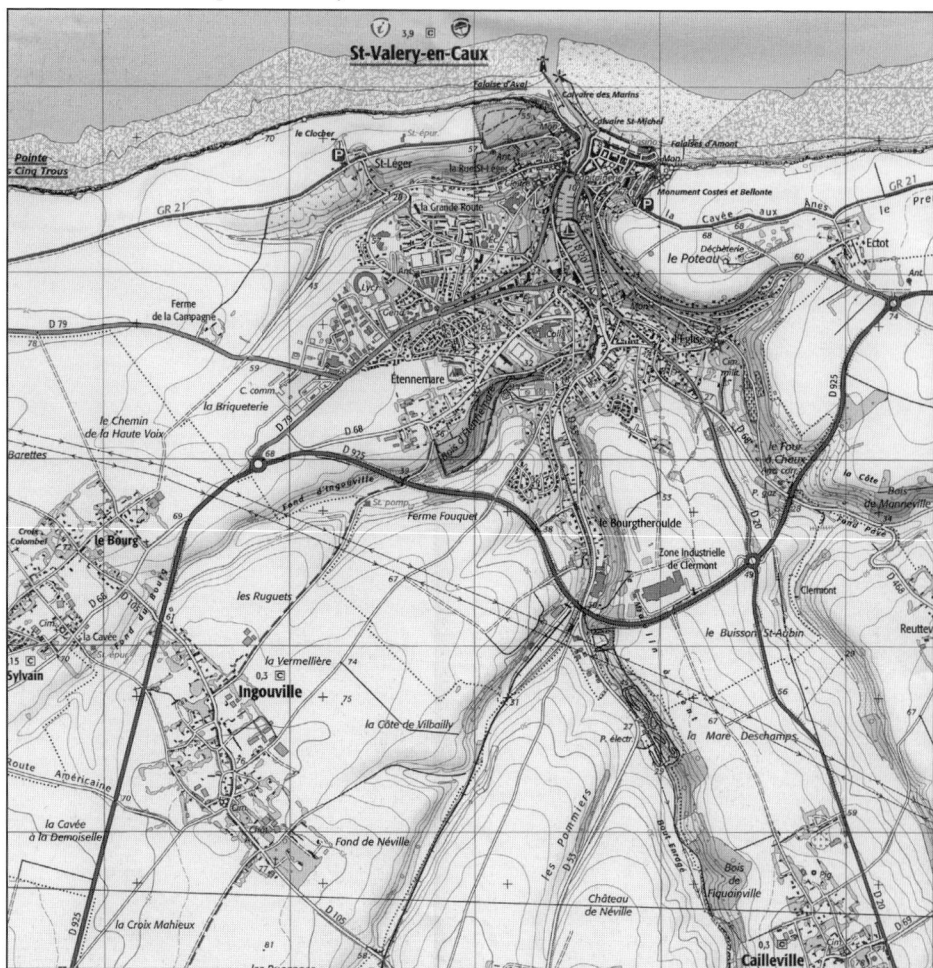

An aerial photograph of St Valery-en-Caux.

the two towns, mainly focused on the war graves and memorials, but twinning was not officially undertaken until 1987. There is a weekly market on Friday and visitors may find parking difficult.

Veules-les-Roses is a tourism and farming village situated on the coast some 12 miles southwest of Dieppe, at the junction of the D68, D926 and the D142 roads. It is approximately 6 miles from St Valery-en-Caux (a ten

A contemporary postcard of Veules-les-Roses.

VEULES-les-ROSES (S.-Inf.) — Vue Générale - Route de Sotteville

minutes drive). The River Veules, which flows through the commune, is the shortest sea-bound river in France, at a mere 1,194 metres. Its water is used to create ponds for growing watercress, from which it finds its way to the sea through a gap in the high chalk cliffs, which overlook a sand and pebble beach.

The beach is not one of the best on the Normandy coast, there are more pebbled areas than sandy patches; but at least there is a beach, located on either side of the white cliffs for which this region is famous. Next to the beach is a paddling pool and children's playground. Veules-les-Roses is one of the oldest villages in the Pays de Caux and it became a popular holiday resort in the nineteenth century, cherished by artistic figures such as Victor Hugo.

The cliffs along this stretch of coast are anything up to 300 feet high.

Acknowledgements

I first acknowledge the numerous soldiers who managed to put their experiences into print for later generations to read, for without them this book would have never been written. To that end I am indebted to Saul David for permission to use his book, *After Dunkirk*, and to quote from the soldier's stories that punctuate it. I must also thank Anette Fuhrmeister of the History Press for giving me permission to use Robert Gardner's *Kensington to St Valery en Caux* and Andrew Bradford's book about his father's escape, *Escape from Saint Valery-en-Caux*. Both of these books have been used to ensure that the chronology in this book on the 51st Division is correct. I must also acknowledge the work of Eric Linklater; his prose has enlightened and delighted me in my quest for information about the 51st (Highland) Division. I must also show my appreciation to Bill Innes for allowing me to quote from his book, *St Valery: The Impossible Odds* and Matt Jones at Pen and Sword for giving permission to quote from Derek Lang's *Return to St Valery* (Leo Cooper).

To my battlefield companions, Paul Webster and Dave Rowland, I am deeply grateful for their input and companionship during the preparation for this book. Dave, for his comments, usually from the back seat of the car and between mouthfuls of something delicious, and Paul, for his measured observations on the whereabouts of Commonwealth war graves and the text of my book. They have both been with me during at least five of the series I have written of the 1940 campaign and have made a valuable contribution.

To my wife Joan I owe an immense 'thank you' for putting up with my constant absences, either in France or in the back bedroom, where I was often to be found tinkering with the text of the latest book. Her support has been invaluable and her comments; although at times her questions have been off the point and more to do with art history, they have usually been sharp and to the point!

Of the institutions that assisted with this book I should mention the help and advice given by The National Archives at Kew and the Imperial War Museum. They have, as always, been most helpful in providing information and directing me to soldiers' accounts of the battles as the 51st Division retreated from the Somme to St Valery-en-Caux.

Much of the information in the book has been sourced from various histories and first-hand accounts; it stands to reason that some of these accounts are at variance with the official version of what took place. Any errors are therefore of my making and I accept full responsibility. I must crave the indulgence of any relative or family member who disagrees with my account of events. Similarly, despite my continuous efforts to contact some copyright holders, I have still been unable to do so. Therefore I must crave the indulgence of those literary executors and publishers and encourage them to get in touch with me through my publisher so that any errors can be rectified.

Chapter 1

The German Order of Battle

The principal formations and units that fought against the 51st (Highland) Division

57th Infantry Division
Created from Bavarian reserve personnel in 1939, it was activated in August 1939. It distinguished itself in southern Poland and during operations on the lower Somme. It was this division that came up against Général de Gaulle during French operations to take the Abbeville bridgehead, in which the French 4th Armoured Division was smashed, along with another French mechanized division. After the fighting in France the 57th Division was stationed in Normandy until April 1941, when it returned to Poland. The Division's commander in 1940 was Lieutenant General Oskar Bluemm, who gave way to General Anton Dostler in September 1941. The Division moved over the River Bresle and Béthune to Dieppe in support of the 11/Motorised Brigade and the 31st Infantry divisions. The Division surrendered to the Russians in May 1945.

31st Infantry Division
Recruited mainly from the Brunswick area, the Division was activated in October 1936 and fought in Poland in 1939. On moving to the Western Front, it was engaged in heavy fighting in Belgium and France during 1940. The Division was present at Veules-les-Roses and St Valery-en-Caux. Its commander in 1940 was Lieutenant General Rudolf Kampfe, who gave way to Kurt Kalmuekoff in May 1941, who was killed in action at Swonco in August 1941. The Division surrendered to the Russians in May 1945.

11th Motorized Brigade (Schützen Brigade)
Commanded by Oberst Günther von Angern, it was responsible for assaulting the 8 and 7/Argyll and Sutherland Highlanders after breaking out of the Abbeville bridgehead. The **12th Infantry Division** was also present and assaulted Oisemont and Amaule before moving on to the Foret d'Eawy. Oberst Günther von Angern was awarded the Knight's Cross during 1940 and promoted to generalleutnant in January 1943. He committed suicide in February 1943 to avoid capture when his formation was encircled by the Russians.

2nd Infantry Division (2nd Motorized Division)
Although Rommel has the commander of the 2nd Motorized Division as General Ludwig Cruewell (*The Rommel Papers*, p. 66) it is probably a

1

(*Left*) Lieutenant General Oskar Bluemm commanded the German 57th Division.
(*Right*) Lieutenant General Rudolf Kampfe commanded the German 31st Division.

Oberst Günther von Angern (far right) commanded the 11th Motorized Brigade.

The 2nd Motorized Division was commanded by Major General Paul Bader.

mistake on his part as in August 1940 Cruewell became commander of the 11th Panzer Division, although some sources have him as commander of the 5th Panzer Division in June 1940. Recruiting its men mainly from the Stettin area, the 2nd Motorized Division was reorganized in 1939 and the 2nd Motorized Infantry Regiment became attached to Wietersheim's XIV Motorized Corps, where it took part in the 'dash to the Channel' and advanced to Dieppe. It was this Division that fought at Huppy. The Division officially became the 12th Panzer Division in January 1941. It was commanded in 1940 by Major General Paul Bader, who gave way to Major General Josef Harpe in October 1940. The Division surrendered to the Russians in May 1945.

5th Panzer Division
Originally a peacetime division, the 5th Panzer Division fought well and was five times awarded a distinguished conduct citation for prowess in combat on the Eastern Front. Organized in 1938, it consisted of a mixture of rifle, artillery and panzer regiments. The Division played a minor and inconspicuous role in the Polish campaign and a more prominent part on the French campaign of 1940. It took part in the conquest of Belgium, the destruction of the French armies around Lille and the capture of Rouen before turning north in the direction of St Valery-en-Caix. The Division was sent to Romania in 1941. In command of the division in 1940 was Lieutenant General Joachim Lemelsen. The Division surrendered to the British in May 1945.

3

(*Left*) Lieutenant General Joachim Lemelsen commanded the 5th Panzer Division. (*Right*) Erwin Rommel commanded the 7th Panzer Division.

7th Panzer Division

Formed at Gera in 1938 as the 2nd Light Division, it became known as the 'Ghost Division' due to its emblem. It initially included the 66/Panzer Battalion and the 5 and 6/Mechanized Cavalry and took part in the invasion of Poland. During the winter of 1939-40 it was converted to a panzer division and added the 25/Panzer Regiment and 7/Rifle Brigade. In February 1940 General Erwin Rommel took over command and the Division broke through Belgium and France, repulsed the major Allied counter-attack at Arras and cut off the escape of the 51st Division. It lost more men than any other German division in the French campaign, with losses that included about forty tanks. Later it overran the French 1st Armoured Division, the 4th North African Division and much of the British 51st Division. Commanders included the 'Desert Fox', Erwin Rommel, who assumed command in February 1940, and Lieutenant General Baron Hans von Funck, who succeeded him in February 1941. The Division surrendered to the British in May 1945.

Fall Rot (Case Red)

The offensive began on Wednesday 5 June and was the successor to *Fall Gelb* in the north of France, which eventually concluded at Dunkirk. The Germans had been planning for a major assault against the Allies south of the Somme since the end of May. Von Brauchitsch, the German Commander in Chief, expected to use his numerical superiority of two to one to break through the Allied line and penetrate deeply behind it. In this he

4

planned correctly. There were 104 German divisions lined up for the attack, against which the allies could only muster forty-nine French divisions, plus of course the British 51st Division and what was left of the 1st Armoured Division. What is a little surprising is that the huge logistic effort required to make *Fall Rot* possible in June 1940 is almost totally ignored in the literature generated by the fall of France and, perhaps for reasons of national honour, it is often written out of French history. [It is worth noting that there is no French Official History for the Second World War, nor is there ever likely to be one.] *Fall Rot* provided a clear display of the ability of the Wehrmacht to manage and adapt, which would be apparent in the remainder of the war. There is little doubt that in May–June 1940, *Fall Rot* was an unprecedented feat of arms.

In addition to the logistical requirements, the Germans had to reorganise and redeploy their forces for the next phase of the campaign. Many of the panzer units were given three or four days rest and by early June were taking up positions in the forward assembly area. Unlike *Fall Gelb* in the north of France, where 70 per cent of the armour came from Army Group A, the panzer divisions were far more evenly distributed for this offensive. One lesson learned from *Fall Gelb* was that the panzer divisions, at times, did not have enough infantry to back them up. This time five motorised corps were formed, each with an accompanying panzer and infantry division. What is perhaps not widely known is that the German high command were well aware of the personal friction between Guderian and Kleist during *Fall Gelb* and decided to promote the often insubordinate Guderian to a panzergruppe commander, an indication, perhaps,

German troops move southwards during *Fall Rot*.

of just how much the Wehrmacht was prepared to tolerate poor and inappropriate behaviour, providing it remained on the winning side!

Despite its deficiencies, the French army was able to develop a reasonable picture of the enemy course of action. By May the *Deuxième Bureau* expected the next phase of the German attack to be a breakout from the Amiens bridgehead and a push towards Reims. In this forecast they were very close to the actual plan for *Fall Rot*. Weygand decided to create a new army group under Huntziger, comprising the Second and Fourth Armies, to block the enemy thrust towards Reims, although, typically, this did not occur until after *Fall Rot* began!

A lesson learnt from the fighting at Sedan was the importance of unity of command in the sector that the Germans chose to make their main effort. Consequently, Weygand upgraded Altmayer's detachment to army status, making it the Tenth Army on 31 May. With this new group Altmayer was expected to contain the enemy bridgeheads over the Somme. As Robert Forczyk wrote in his book *Case Red*, 'unlike the opening shots of the campaign, the Wehrmacht would no longer enjoy operational surprise; the French knew how and where they were going to attack'. Many historians still believe that if the French had had some sort of coherent, effective, command structure it would have delayed, if not halted, the German advance. We shall never know.

Chapter 2

The British Forces

Some of the units that fought with, or were assigned to, the 51st (Highland) Division

A division such as the 51st (Highland) Division was the principal formation of the British Army and numbered between 12,000 and 18,000 men, although in this case, after it was strengthened, it numbered nearer 21,000. The division was an all arms formation, consisting principally of infantry, armour, artillery, engineer and signals units and was commanded by a major general. During the First World War the division was organized into twelve battalions of infantry, four battalions to a brigade; but by 1918, owing to manpower shortages, the division was reduced to nine battalions, with three battalion to a brigade.

The smallest element in a battalion was the **section**, which at the beginning of the Second World War comprised eight men but by 1945 had increased to ten men. The section was usually commanded by a corporal. Three sections formed a **platoon**, commanded either by a second lieutenant or lieutenant. At the beginning of the Second World War a platoon was sometimes commanded by a platoon sergeant major, with the rank of WO III; and some platoons were designated Mortar and Carrier Platoons. As regards **companies**, most infantry battalions were made up of four rifle companies as well as a headquarters company, and was usually commanded by a captain or major. The support company only came into existence in 1944. The **battalion** was made up of five companies and commanded by a lieutenant colonel and usually formed part of a brigade. The **brigade** could operate independently, as indeed could a battalion, and was made up of all arms and was commanded by a brigadier. Three brigades made up a division. Infantry brigades of the 51st Division were made up of the following sub units:

Infantry
152 Brigade was commanded by Brigadier Herbert Stewart, who was hit by shrapnel at Forêt d'Eu on 5 June and evacuated from St Valery, command devolving to Lieutenant Colonel Ian Barclay of the 2/Seaforth Highlanders. Command of the 2/Seaforths in turn devolved to the second in command after Barclay was appointed to fill the gap left by Stewart. However, the strain of constant withdrawal proved too much for the second in command, and Major James Murray Grant eventually took over and became its *de facto* commander. The 4/Seaforth Highlanders commanding

(Left) James Murray Grant became the *de facto* commander of the 2/Seaforths. *(Right)* Ronnie Macintosh-Walker took over command of the 4/Camerons from the Earl of Cawdor. He is pictured as a captain in 1934.

officer, Lieutenant Colonel Harry Houldsworth, was wounded on 4 June and replaced by Major Ian Shaw-Mackenzie. Finally, the 4/Queen's Own Cameron Highlander's commanding officer, John Duncan Campbell, the 5th Earl of Cawdor, was replaced by Major Ronnie Mackintosh-Walker in June 1940. Mackintosh-Walker was a regular officer who had arrived the day before with 900 reinforcements. Barclay, Shaw-Mackenzie, James Murray Grant and Mackintosh-Walker were all taken prisoner at St Valery-en-Caux.

153 Brigade was commanded by Brigadier George Burney, who died on 7 November 1940 aged 51years whilst he was a prisoner in captivity. The three infantry battalions in 153 Brigade were the 4/Black Watch, commanded by Lieutenant Colonel Rory Macpherson, the 1/Gordon Highlanders, commanded by Lieutenant Colonel Harry Wright and the 5/Gordon Highlanders under the command of Lieutenant Colonel Alick Buchanan-Smith, who was replaced initially by his second in command and then by Lieutenant Colonel 'Sailor' Clark on 20 May. Burney was taken prisoner at St Valery.

154 Brigade was commanded by Brigadier Arthur Stanley-Clarke. Its three infantry battalions consisted of the 1/Black Watch, commanded by Lieutenant Colonel Eric Honeyman, who had replaced Lieutenant Colonel 'Steve' Stephen. The 7/Argyll and Sutherland Highlanders were

(*Left*) Lieutenant Colonel Alick Buchanan-Smith commanded the 5/Gordons but ran foul of Brigadier Burney and was eventually replaced by Lieutenant Colonel 'Sailor' Clark on 20 May 1940. He retired as a brigadier and was created Baron Balerno in 1963 for his services to education and politics. (*Right*) Lieutenant Colonel Eric Honeyman replaced Lieutenant Colonel Steve Stephen after the latter became ill.

commanded by Lieutenant Colonel Edmund Buchanan, who was taken prisoner at Franleu; and the 8/Argyll and Sutherland Highlanders were commanded by Lieutenant Colonel Hamish Grant. Stanley-Clarke escaped captivity by going south with Ark Force.

Armoured Units

The armoured units of the BEF in 1940 consisted of mechanized cavalry units of the 51st Division, such as the 1/Lothian and Border Yeomanry and the battalions of the Royal Tank Regiment. Although the **1st Armoured Division** was not a part of the 51st Division as such, it worked with the Highlanders during operations during the battle for Abbeville and has therefore been included. It is interesting that at no time during the 1st Armoured Division's creation was the opinion of an individual familiar with tanks sought; and when the time came for selecting its commander, the most experienced man in the British Army, Major General Percy Hobart, was passed over in favour of Major General Roger Evans, a former Royal Horse Guards officer. The 1st Armoured Division had already given up two of its support battalions and a brigade of tanks to the defence of Calais and never really recovered. Had the Division been at full strength and in particular used in large scale counter-attacks to break the advancing Panzer Divisions, the story of the battle might have been different. As it was, the Division was placed under the command of the French and was chosen to be the spearhead of an attack on 27 May.

The 2nd Armoured Brigade launched their assault into a maelstrom of fire at Huppy. The Bays, attacking to the left of the Hussars, were mauled by the German gunners. In a lesson the British were to learn again at great cost in the Western Desert, frontal attacks by armour, particularly lightly armoured vehicles, against well handled and dug in anti-tank defences were a recipe for disaster. In a similar manner during the First World War it was discovered that cavalry action against well sited machine guns was also a recipe for disaster.

The attack itself was almost a complete rout. The 3rd Tank Brigade made better headway, but without infantry to hold the territory gained, they had to withdraw in the face of pressure from the defending Germans. After the attack of 27 May the Composite Regiment was loaned to the 51st Division to increase the striking power of the 1/Lothians and thereafter to reinforce the Support Group south of Aumale. The Division was used piecemeal for various actions; but any defensive preparations the Division was about to make were abruptly halted by news of an imminent French armistice.

The 3rd Armoured Brigade had arrived at Cherbourg by the evening of 17 June, was loaded on to the waiting ships and left as soon as possible. The Brigade's evacuation was just two days ahead of the arrival in the port of German forces under Rommel. Their progress had been delayed by the valiant stand of the 51st (Highland) Division. Thus the Brigade's escape was very much a close run thing. The 2nd Armoured Brigade travelled to a different port for its evacuation, namely Brest in Brittany. At this stage, the formation only had fifteen tanks, which had been loaded on to railcars for transport to Brest, but never arrived. The remaining men of the 2nd Brigade arrived back in England without their much needed tanks.

The **1st Armoured Division** consisted of 257 tanks, of which the main battle tank in the 2nd (Light) Armoured Brigade was the Vickers Mk VIB and VIC and were already very much outdated by the types of German armour. Added to this the new BESA machine guns had only recently arrived and they were still mostly in their cases, unpacked and unready.

The 3rd Armoured Brigade was for the most part equipped with the Cruiser tank, with a mixture of types: the A9 Cruiser Mk I, the A10 Cruiser Mk II, the A13 Cruiser Mk II and the A13 Cruiser Mk IV. Designated the heavy brigade and consisting of the 2nd and 5th Royal Tank Regiment, the A13 Cruiser tank was armed with a 2 pounder gun. Each tank battalion was equipped with fifty-two tanks, ten armoured scout cars and was organized into a headquarters, a headquarters squadron and three squadrons. The Brigade was commanded by Brigadier John Crocker.

The three regiments of the 2nd Armoured Brigade, 10/Royal Hussars, 2/Dragoon Guards (Queen's Bays) and 9/Queen's Royal Lancers, were each equipped with fifty-eight light tanks and five armoured scout carriers.

A Vickers Mk VIB light tank.

The Brigade was organized into a headquarters, a headquarters squadron and three squadrons and was commanded by Brigadier Richard McCreery.

The 1/Lothians and Border Regiment, the cavalry reconnaissance regiment attached to the 51st Division, was originally the 1/Fife and Forfar Yeomanry but was replaced by the 1/Lothians and Border Regiment. Both regiments were Territorial but the 1/Lothian seemed to have gained in efficiency after the appointment of Lieutenant Colonel Mike Ansell as

An A13 Cruiser tank.

(*Left*) Roger MacCreery, commander of the 2nd Armoured Brigade. (*Right*) Brigadier John Crocker, commander of the 3rd Armoured Brigade.

The 1st Armoured Division was under the direction of Major General Roger Evans (on the right). He is pictured here with John Crocker in 1945.

Commanding Officer and was referred to by fellow Yeomanry regiments as the 'Loathsome and Bloody' regiment. Eric Linklater, author of *The Highland Division*, was predisposed enough to write of Ansell that he had a kind of genius for suddenly appearing in the very place where he was needed: a fine accolade indeed. A reconnaissance regiment, such as the 1/Lothians in 1940, was equipped with twenty-eight Mk VIB light tanks with armaments of .5 and .303 machine guns. The tanks itself had a very thin skin of 14mm of armour and could muster forty mph. In addition there were forty-four Bren gun carriers, each of which carried a light machine gun and a crew of three.

Lieutenant Colonel Mike Ansell, taken in 1924.

Artillery

The Artillery Field Regiment was organized into a headquarters and two batteries of twelve guns, as was the case of the 17 (Highland), 23 (Highland) and 75 (Highland) Field Regiments. The 17 and 23 were regular, while the 75/Field Regiment was a Territorial unit. 1/Royal Horse Artillery from April 1940 was attached to the Division, as was the 51 (West Highland) Anti-Tank Regiment. This was a Territorial unit and was converted from 54/Field Regiment in November 1938. The regiment had a headquarters and four batteries of twelve 2-pounder guns. 204 Battery of the 51/Anti-Tank Regiment escaped via Ark Force, as did the 51 Medium Regiment RA (TA.) Both the 17th and 75th Field Regiments escaped the clutches of Erwin Rommel and were evacuated with Ark Force at Le Havre, while the 23rd Field Regiment was captured at St Valery-en-Caux.

Pioneers

Although two battalions, 7/Royal Norfolks and the 6/Royal Scots, were designated pioneer battalions, they were quite capable of fighting as infantry and, indeed, the 7/Royal Norfolks did so at St Valery-en-Caux and other places along the route of the retreat. The 7/Battalion, Royal Norfolk Regiment was formed in May 1939 as a 2nd Line Territorial Army duplicate of the 5/Battalion and, therefore, contained many former members of the 5/Battalion. Together with the 5th and 6th battalions, the 7th was assigned to the 53rd Infantry Brigade, part of the 18th Infantry Division, until November 1939, when it assigned to pioneer duties in France with the British Expeditionary Force (BEF). In May 1940, it was re-assigned to the 51st (Highland) Infantry Division. Only thirty-one members of the battalion managing to return to Britain; the Battalion's

CO, Lieutenant Colonel Archie Debenham, was taken prisoner along with his second in command, Major Gordon Johnson, at St Valery-en-Caux. Lieutenant Colonel Thomas Corbett, 2nd Baron Rowallan, commanded the 6/ Royal Scots Fusiliers and escaped via Ark Force. (In 1945, the Boy Scouts Association appointed him as its Chief Scout of the United Kingdom and Chief Scout of the Commonwealth in April, appointments he retained until 1959.)

A photograph of Lieutenant Colonel Thomas Corbett, 2nd Baron Rowallan, taken when he was Chief Scout in 1950. He was commander of the 6/Royal Scots Fusiliers in France during 1940.

Machine Gun Battalions

Both the 1/Princess Louise's Kensington Regiment and the 7/Royal Northumberland Fusiliers were machine gun battalions of the Territorial Army. The Kensington Regiment was originally the 13th County of London Battalion and was affiliated to the Middlesex Regiment from 1916. In 1937, with the break-up of the London Regiment, this unit adopted the title The Princess Louise's Kensington Regiment, The Middlesex Regiment. In common with the 7/Royal Northumberland Fusiliers, each battalion was organized into five companies, a headquarters company and four machine gun companies equipped with twelve water-cooled .303 Vickers machine guns. Each machine-gun company was divided into three platoons of four guns, with each platoon sub-divided into two sections of two guns. It was said that the Vickers once fired continuously, without interruption, for seven days. There is little evidence for this but, if true, represented a considerable feat of arms. Mind you, the expenditure of ammunition would have been colossal! In addition to the forty-eight Vickers machine guns, each battalion had eighteen Bren guns as well as personal weapons. The full complement was about 740 officers and men and was commanded by a lieutenant colonel. The function of a machine gun battalion was to provide additional fire to the infantry units, which meant that in practice the Kensingtons and Northumberland Fusiliers hardly ever fought as a single unit of four companies. Units, usually of company strength, would be scattered around a brigade or division, depending on where they were most needed. Eric Linklater felt that both battalions were worthy of commendation:

> The two machine gun battalions, Northumberland Fusiliers and Kensingtons, were for tactical purposes divided amongst the brigades, and because they did not fight as a whole it is difficult to assess or describe their work. But wherever the infantry were in action there were machine gunners to support them, and perhaps it is sufficient to say that the battalions which had the Kensingtons attached to them speak well of them, while those which were assisted by the Northumberland Fusiliers were convinced that they had better support. The conclusion is that both were good.

The Commanding Officer of the Kensingtons was Lieutenant Colonel Gordon Parker, a regular soldier from the Middlesex Regiment, who took over from Lieutenant Colonel Howard in April 1940. Lieutenant Colonel Geoffrey Fenwicke-Clennell was CO of the 7/Northumberland Fusiliers. He was taken prisoner at St Valery-en-Caux; but Gordon Parker escaped via Ark Force with HQ, B and C Companies.

The Beauman Division

The Lines of Communication nearest the Somme comprised all the area between the Somme and the Seine and was under the command of

Brigadier Archibald Beauman, who had his Headquarters at Rouen. The administration of the whole Lines of Communication was conducted from a château near Le Mans and was under the command of Major General Phillip de Fonblanque. Beauman's responsibility was to safeguard the area against aerial and ground attack. Towards the end of May, when the Germans had reached the Somme, it became necessary to form a defence force. Reinforcement camps and base details in the area were thoroughly combed for all available troops; but Beauman quickly realized that such a small force was quite inadequate to safeguard the huge store depots in his area and he needed to raise more troops. In so doing he instructed **Colonel John Diggle**, who commanded the Pioneer battalions, to equip them as a fighting force. The 2,500 men that Diggle put together were positioned along the River Andelle.

From the three main reinforcement depots in the Rouen area, Beauman cobbled together five battalions, who took in the names of their commanding officers, Perowne, Wait, Ray, Davie and Meredith. The whole force was placed under the command of **Colonel Charles Vicary**, the BEF's Reinforcement Officer, and was positioned between the headwaters of the Rivers Béthune and Andelle. To cover the approaches to the Seine the sectors were placed under Royal Engineers officers: the Béthune sector under Colonel Doyle, the centre sector under Colonel Amis and the Andelle sector under Colonel White. The responsibility of these officers was to ensure that every bridge and culvert was prepared for demolition and that roadblocks were put up at each tactical point.

This motley force, eventually numbering about 8,000 men, advanced some 27 miles north-east of Rouen and was strung out along 57 miles of

The Beauman Brigade was poorly armed but they managed to hold up enemy forces for a week or more. This photograph was taken in March 1940, probably on manoeuvers on the Somme.

Brigadier Archibald Beauman, photographed in 1921 when he was a lieutenant colonel.

front, following the line of the River Béthune from Dieppe through Neufchâtel and southwards to the Forêt de Lyons. Though thinly held, the front managed to hold up enemy forces for a week or more. Even for a regular formation their performance would have been regarded as magnificent; and when it is considered that this force had only been thrown together a few days previously, their battlefield behaviour can only be described in superlatives. In June 'A' Brigade of the Beauman Division, commanded by Brigadier Michael Green, was sent to the 51st Division to assist it in holding the Bresle; it consisted of the 4/Buffs, the 1/5 Foresters and the 4/Border Regiment.

Chapter 3

From Scotland to the Saar

On 9 May 1940 the British Army in France was over 300,000 strong and was holding the so-called Gort Line, a name taken from the Commander-in-Chief of the BEF, Lord Gort. The line ran for some 30 miles north and south of Lille and along the Belgian border. The Lines of Communication, through which the army was fed and supplied with necessary stores, ammunition and reinforcements, extended along the Atlantic coast of France to the ports of Brest, St Nazaire, Le Havre and Cherbourg.

At first light on 10 May the German armies, with very little warning, invaded the Low Countries. Automatically, Plan D, a scheme instigated by the French, saw the Allied forces take up their defensive positions along the River Dyle in Belgium in the vicinity of Louvain, abandoning the Gort Line, a line between Belgium and France that the British troops had spent all winter fortifying. The whole operation was carried out so smoothly that it almost seemed if the Allied armies were being encouraged to vacate the Gort Line by an enemy that had another plan up its sleeve. How right they were. The other plan became apparent a few days later when German armoured forces smashed through the Ardennes at Sedan and quickly formed a wedge between the British and French armies.

It was a development that caught the French by surprise and exposed the right flank of the British Expeditionary Force, forcing them to withdraw. The German armies were unstoppable and swept like a scythe around the rear of the allies in the north, communication between Lord Gort, the British Commander-in-Chief, and the French Grand Quartier Général (CQG) was interrupted and made worse by elements of the 2nd Panzer Division reaching the sea at Noyelles sur Mer, near St-Valery sur Somme, on 20 May, thereby isolating the French forces and the BEF from their counterparts south of the River Somme. As the BEF became more isolated it was gradually forced back towards the sea and the danger of encirclement and capture became a reality. It became clear that the only way out of this dilemma was by way of the beaches in the neighbourhood of Dunkerque. This happened on 26 May when the evacuation, codenamed *Dynamo*, was given the go-ahead and orders were sent to Vice Admiral Bertrand Ramsey in Dover to assume overall command of the operation. Gort estimated that perhaps 30,000 or 40,000 could be evacuated but in the event, miraculously as it turned out, over 300,000 British and French troops escaped captivity in an evacuation that was hailed optimistically as a victory.

John Vereker, 6th Lord Gort.

The formations assigned to the BEF were those from the Regular Army and included some of the senior regiments of the day. The first to move on the outbreak of war were the four senior regular divisions; the first Territorial Army (TA) Division (48th (South Midland)) did not arrive until January 1940. Thus the BEF had been in France from September 1939, a period of time dubbed the 'Phoney War' due to its lack of engagement with the enemy, and it was only in the last few weeks before the evacuation from Dunkerque that the Army was in action. In those last few weeks from 10 May the ground forces fought a fierce and unrelenting battle with the enemy across a wide area. Colour Sergeant Gregor Macdonald of the 4/Cameron Highlanders remembered the armada of German aircraft flying over his position on the Saar on 10 May:

We were standing at first light when we heard the steady drone of aircraft and shortly afterwards the sky was dark with enemy bombers flying due west at a height of around 4,000 feet. For the next two hours we counted wave after wave of Junkers and Fockers flying due

Vice Admiral Bertram Ramsey. Pictured here as an admiral in 1944.

west without any fighter cover. This was not surprising as we had not seen a British of French aircraft in the sky since out arrival in France three months before.

The bombers Macdonald had seen were in all probability Heinkels and Dorniers; but the 10 May indeed heralded the start of the long awaited German invasion.

South of the River Somme, having been transported from the Maginot Line (the Saar region) by an extremely roundabout route, the 51st (Highland) Division found themselves cut off from the bulk of the British Army by German armoured forces and were now under the command of the

French Tenth Army. With no hope of moving north across the River Somme, the Division settled down with some reluctance to bolstering the defence of the River Somme crossings with their allies.

The 51st (Highland) Division

In September 1939 the 51st Division was a TA Division of three brigades, consisting of such famous regiments as the Black Watch, Seaforth Highlanders, Gordon Highlanders, Cameron Highlanders and the Argyll and Sutherland Highlanders. In addition the infantry brigades were supported by other units, such as engineers, artillery, signals and three field ambulance units. Its General Officer Commanding (GOC) was 56-year-old Major General Victor Fortune, a man who had fought with the Black Watch, rising to become one of the regiment's commanding officers, during the Battle of the Somme in the First World War. During that service Fortune was awarded the Distinguished Service Order, was twice mentioned in dispatches; he was appointed GOC of the 51st Division in 1937. He was reputed to be the only officer that served with the Division throughout the war that remained unwounded.

When the Division assembled in Scotland in 1938 for preliminarily training, weapons were in short supply and many of the men were still in uniforms of 1918 vintage or in civilian clothes. Modern military kit in the form of uniforms and weapons could be rectified, but for many in the Division worse was still to come. In September 1939 the kilt was seen to be unsuited to the increased mechanization of modern warfare and was

Major General Victor Fortune (holding the chart), pictured at Caudray on 8 June.

British troops (probably those of the 51st Division) engaging in bayonet practise. Note their civilian clothes.

destined to be replaced by the Battle Dress, a two piece khaki uniform that initially developed a gap between the blouse and trousers which would open up in extreme movement as the buttons popped. It was seen as an attack on the very item of uniform that had given the Division the nickname, 'Ladies from Hell'. The Commanding Officer of the 5/Gordons was so incensed by this directive that he held a parade on the square at Bordon Camp, Hampshire, in January 1940, during which a single kilt was ceremonially burned. He is on record as saying that, 'For 200 years the English had wanted to take the kilt away from the Highlanders and now they had succeeded'. However, despite the War Office directive, many men of the Division clung onto their kilts, taking the banned item to France with them. It is true to say that the 51st Division largely ignored the order and contemporary photographs depict a number of those men who fought as part of the rearguard at St Valery-en-Caux wearing their kilts proudly until their release from captivity in 1945. In fact, on arrival in the Saar, Lieutenant Noel Jardine-Patterson, the 1/Black Watch Signals Officer, reported that 'every other officer seemed to be wearing a kilt or trews' (close-fitting tartan trousers).

Kilt or not, the relentless cycle of training continued. Moving south to the Aldershot area, Corporal Jock Cairns of 16 Platoon, 8/Argyll and Sutherland Highlanders, later wrote that he had never crawled through so much wet grass and English heather as he did at Aldershot! Whether he wore a kilt is not recorded. In January 1940 the Division sailed for France, landing at Le Havre. In France further training took place during one of

23

Trying on gasmasks.

the worst winters on record and on 28 March the Division moved to join the rest of the BEF between Bailleul and Armentières, close to the Belgian border. Training continued without a break but was combined with daily toil on the Gort Line, in effect, an elaborate ditch extending the Maginot Line, with its chain of fortresses and bunkers, along the border with Belgium. Unfortunately for the Allies, Belgium was neutral and, until Germany trampled through the country, Allied troops were unlikely to be invited across the border. In the event the whole exercise turned out to be for nothing as the Allied armies never stood to defend this line as the invasion by Germany prompted a mass movement to the line of the River Dyle, on the assumption that, as in 1914, the Germans would attack through Belgium.

The Saar

On 13 April, one month before the Germans launched their attack, it was decided by General Headquarters (GHQ) that the 51st Division would take over a sector on the Saar front in the area of Hombourg-Budange. Before departure Army Command, in their wisdom, decided to stiffen up the Division with professionals, principally as French divisions were a little larger than their British counterparts; but they also took advantage of the fact that there were too many territorial units in the division. Consequently the 6/Seaforths, Gordons and Black Watch were replaced with regular

24

battalions, resulting in the 2/Seaforths, 1/Gordons and 1/Black Watch joining 152, 153 and 154 Brigades. To strengthen the artillery, 76 and 77/Field Regiments were replaced with the regular soldiers of 17 and 23/Field Regiments and 283/Field Company of the Royal Engineers were exchanged for the regular 26/Field Company. The 1/Lothian and Border Horse replaced the 1/Fife and Forfar Yeomanry as the light armoured regiment. In effect the Division had become the strongest division in the British Army, with a complement of around 21,000 men.

It is hard to see how this 'professional exchange' was expected to work in practice without a closer integration of TA and regular soldiers in a mixed battalion, as each unit was essentially a separate entity. Robert Gardner, writing in *Kensington to St-Valery en Caux*, felt it was 'part of an unjustifiable prejudice on the part of GHQ against TA units'; in this he may well have been correct. Lord Kitchener in the Great War harboured a similar, unfair, discrimination against the Territorial battalions and the sentiment may well have continued into the next war.

Certainly the purge of Territorial officers continued with the appointment of Lieutenant Colonel Mike Ansell to command the 1/Lothian and Border Horse (LBH) and culminated with Major Ronnie Mackintosh-Walker taking over command of the 4/Cameron Highlanders in June 1940 from John Campbell, the 5th Earl of Cawdor, who was sent home to rest after being 'worn out'.

The 1/Black Watch, now with 152 Brigade, had already been on a tour of duty with the French 12 Brigade in the area over the previous Christmas and was therefore familiar with the rather indifferent French arrangements when it came to the enemy. Since early in December 1939 British infantry brigades had been sent to this front to gain valuable combat experience against German troops and since the end of March 1940 the French High Command had agreed to extending the sector in order the hasten the battle hardening of the BEF. French divisions were, on the whole, larger than the British, consequently the 51st Division would be strengthened by two pioneer battalions, the 7/Royal Norfolks and the 6/Royal Scots Fusiliers, together with two machine gun battalions, the 1/Princess Louise's Kensington Regiment and 7/Royal Northumberland Fusiliers, plus additional artillery and engineers.

Fighting on the Saar
The plan was for 154 Brigade to move into the original British sector, with 153 and 153 Brigades moving into position on either side. To the north of the sector was the French 2nd Division and to the south the French 42nd Division. Here the Division was under French command and Major General Fortune was told it would be a short attachment. Had he but known what was to take place he might have voiced his reservations a little more loudly. By 1 May the Division had taken over positions from the French and were settling into their new home.

One of the forts on the Maginot Line. Britsh troops are seen marching across the moat.

The British were immediately disappointed, not only with the poor quality of the French accommodation but the distinct lack of spirit demonstrated by their Allies. They quickly discovered that the much publicized Maginot Line was not a solid line of defence but a series of (generally) underground gun emplacements in the form of forts. The distances between the forts was sometimes up to 5 miles and in between were blockhouses, barbed wire and anti-tank obstacles. The British Division was assigned to *La Couverture*, which was put out in front of the forts to prevent the enemy from making any close investigation of the elaborate fortifications. In addition there were supposed to be four further defensive lines of defence. The first of these, about 3 miles behind the forts, was the *Ligne d'Arrêt*, or Stop Line. This was meant to be the final 'backstop' position but had yet to be completed. In front of the forts was the *Ligne de Recueil* or Recoil Line, followed by the *Ligne de Soutien*, a non continuous line that did not feature in the 51st Divisional sector. Finally there was the *Ligne de Contact* or Outpost Line, situated only a short distance from the German border and some 7 miles in front of the forts. The line was intended to delay the advance of German forces and had, in addition, several small fortified positions and faced the German Siegfried Line. The sector of the *Ligne de Contact* to be taken over from the French ran from

26

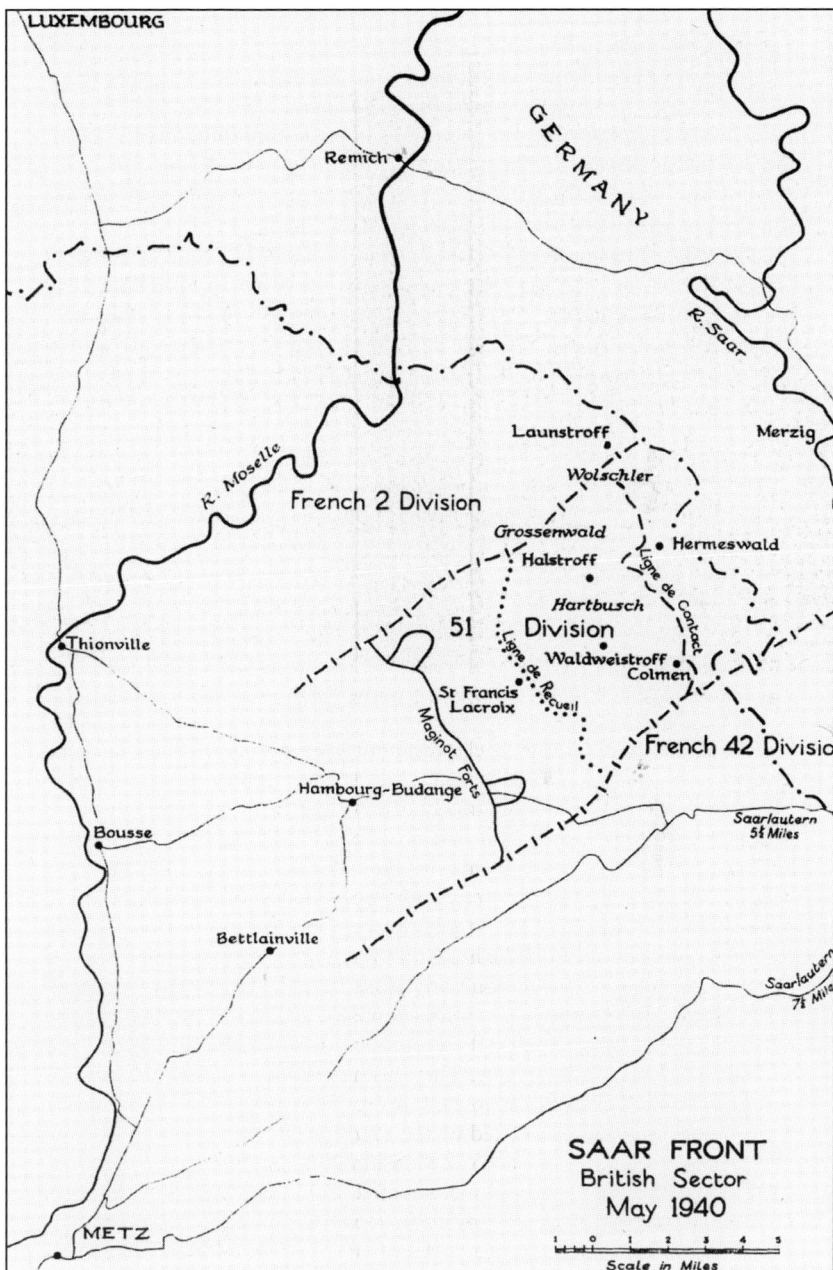

LUXEMBOURG

GERMANY

Remich

R. Saar

R. Moselle

Launstroff

Merzig

Wolschler

French 2 Division

Grossenwald

Hermeswald

Halstroff

Ligne de Contact

Hartbusch

51 Division

Thionville

Waldweistroff

Colmen

Ligne de Recueil

St Francis
Lacroix

French 42 Divisio

Maginot Forts

Hambourg-Budange

Saarlautern
5¼ Miles

Bousse

Bettlainville

Saarlautern
7¼ Miles

SAAR FRONT
British Sector
May 1940

METZ

1 0 1   2   3   4   5
Scale in Miles

The region occupied by the 51st (Highland) Division on the Saar.

27

Heydwald Wood to Wolschler, Grossenwald, Grindorf, Hartbuch, Colmen and Niunkirchen.

The *Ligne de Contact* was at this point 10 miles east of the Maginot forts. Military maps of the area between the Maginot Line and the German border indicated close contour lines and swathes of deciduous forest dominated by the vastness of the Forêt Domaniale de Kalenhofen. The area close to the German border was a forested landscape, with small villages and farms connected by tracks through the woods.

Each military unit taking over the ground from another would undoubtedly find a number of things they would change, but the speed at which the French vacated their positions dumbfounded the relieving Scotsmen. Corporal Jock Cairns, an 8/Argyll and Sutherland Highlanders NCO, had little patience with the French, particularly their apparent disregard of the closeness of the enemy:

> Our platoon was to be manning a low wooded hill; across the valley there were similar features and a steep track leading to a village. On our arrival the French seem to be delighted to be relieved, and despite the darkness, lit up cigarettes and were very noisy and seemed anxious to leave immediately, as they had been expecting an attack. Platoon HQ, with Lieutenant Douglas (Sholto Douglas of later Norwegian SOE fame), seemed to have lost themselves in the darkness. Our section was lost for words, especially when we saw how quickly the French were dashing off. In my scholastic French I asked the French officer if he would oblige us by leaving one of his heavy machine guns on loan. He did so with a large supply of magazines and ammunition.

The 4/Camerons take over a section on the Maginot Line from the French.

His sergeant cheered us up no end when he said, 'You will need it all, as the Boche will know there is a new lot taking over'. If the Boche didn't know before, they knew now, as the French rapidly departed, smoking and singing noisily. Then the sergeant dashed back and shouted in a voice that the enemy must have heard, The Boche will test you out shortly. *Bonne chance*!

Lieutenant Colonel Stephen, the commanding officer of the 1/Black Watch at the time, was equally unimpressed by the attitude of the French division they were to relieve:

The impression one got from the French was of complete inertia. They were fed up with being in the line, very jumpy and glad to get away. The whole idea appeared to be that directly the Germans attacked they would withdraw behind the fortress area; but it was never laid down what constituted an attack and how much resistance they would show. On the other hand the British troops were determined to teach the enemy a lesson and make any advance as costly as possible.

In fact many of the Highlanders were surprised to discover the French soldiers had an unofficial arrangement with the Germans to reduce the degree of warlike behaviour and to conduct activities in a relatively peaceful manner with each other. This was especially true in the area manned by the French 102/Regiment, where little firing took place and ration trucks were allowed unmolested access between 10.00am and 4.00pm. This state of affairs ended on 1 May when the Germans became aware that new troops

German troops advancing.

Men of the 7/Royal Northumberland Fusiliers with a .303 Vickers machine gun.

were facing them; Headquarters 154 Brigade reported a very disturbed night, with a great deal of shooting and artillery fire.

The Kensington Regiment arrived in the assembly area of Talange on 28 April. Their Commanding Officer, Lieutenant Colonel Gordon Parker, took advantage of the lull to reconnoitre the operational areas allocated to 152, 153 and 154 Brigades and decided that two of the battalion's four machine gun platoons would be deployed in the forward area at any one time with the remaining two held in reserve. C and D Companies were the first to go forward. The same arrangement was adopted by the 7/Royal Northumberland Fusiliers, with inter-company reliefs carried out on a frequent basis.

On 10 May the front line battalions were the 4/Camerons (152 Brigade), the 1/Black Watch (154 Brigade) and the 4/Black Watch (153 Brigade). Elements of the Lothian and Border Horse were also in the line, with three light tanks supporting each brigade, while the carrier personnel carried out infantry duty.

13 May

Up until 12 May enemy activity against the division had been confined to small scale attacks against forward positions. However, on 13 May this all changed when German ground forces launched a major assault against two

30

Highland brigades and the flanking French troops. The thought that what appeared at first to be an engagement between two patrols was banished and two hours later heavy shelling of the front line began, especially intense in the areas occupied by 153 and 154 Brigades. At Battalion Headquarters of the 1/Black Watch signal flares were spotted from the forward position of both flanking companies, D Company, in particular, called for defensive fire though rifle and Bren-gun fire ensured that the enemy did not advance too far. Captain Patrick Campell-Preston, commanding D Company, summed up the fighting in his sector, which was dubbed, by those that fought on 13 May, as the Battle of Rémeling:

> This particular attack near the village of Bettling was repulsed. The Germans suffered heavy casualties, with 2/Lt John Moon's platoon along claiming at least forty Germans killed. 1/Black Watch losses were a mere five dead and eight wounded. The Germans had attacked with hugely superior numbers and were supported by eight artillery batteries compared to three supporting the Black Watch. To the left of the 1st Battalion the 4/Black Watch, however, faced an even sterner task. 153 Brigade had had some two weeks less in which to strengthen the defences that their French predecessors had largely ignored. Nevertheless, the German assault was repulsed.

When ammunition supplies were running low, tanks of No. 1 Troop of the Lothian and Border Horse arrived with fresh supplies, which were issued with some difficulty to the forward posts. Such was the ferocity of the defence that the Germans admitted defeat and called off their attack. But the hammer-blow that fell on their neighbours the 4/Black Watch, was considerably heavier; and, as Lieutenant Colonel Rory Macpherson, the CO of the 4/Black Watch, pointed out, the defences available to the other battalions in the British Sector were infinitely superior to those of the 4/Black Watch. Consequently they were to suffer more heavily in the artillery bombardment and subsequent assault. Casualties incurred on the 4/Black Watch for 13 May were six killed, twenty-five wounded and approximately thirty taken prisoner.

Pressure had been exerted on all the front line battalions, each of which inflicted heavy toll on their attackers; the gunner regiments did fine work disrupting attacks and causing heavy casualties amongst the enemy.

14 May

Early on 14 May the Gordon Highlanders were subjected to a heavy bombardment and some 3,600 shells landed on one company alone, cutting telephone cables and flattening defensive positions. After the bombardment came the infantry; but the defenders were far from being shocked into submission and during the fight that ensued the Gordons fought them off. The 7/Argylls, who relieved the 1/Black Watch, also fought off a determined attack and in front of their positions lay the bodies of thirteen

The German Army could call up the Junkers 87 Squadrons at almost any time to support them.

of the enemy. This coincided with a serious breakdown in relations between Brigadier George Burney and the 42 years-old Buchanan-Smith, the 5/Gordon Highlanders Commanding Officer. Lance Corporal George Maclennan, a medic, witnessed the showdown between Burney and Buchanan-Smith:

> Brigadier Burney arrived and ordered our CO to send all his carriers and two companies into Rémleing to help the Black Watch withdraw. Buchanan-Smith replied, and I was there with the doctor when he said this, 'Rémeling is one of the most stupid positions any men could be in. This battalion is like my family. When I go up I'm going with the whole battalion. I'm not sending up part of it to be sacrificed.' It was at this point that Burney threatened him with a court-martial and in the end he was forced to send up the carriers and one company. But he was right all along, it was a stupid position.

On 15 May Buchanan-Smith was replaced by his second in command, Major Rupert Christie, which left the Earl of Cawdor as the only remaining territorial officer commanding an infantry battalion in the Division. On one hand Buchanan-Smith could have rephrased his comments about Rémeling but Burney, it seems, was determined to replace him with a regular officer. Presumably this change in command was done with the approval of Victor Fortune; but whatever the arguments for and against, the outcome was destined to result in Buchanan-Smith being relieved of his command. He returned home to become Director of the Selection of Personnel in the War Office.

15 May

Just before dawn on 15 May the shelling intensified in Heywald Wood and communications between Company HQ and the forward platoons were broken. The 5/Gordon Highlanders D Company, under Captain Lawrie, despite repeated attempts to reach his men, finally sent a message to

German soldiers preparing for battle.

Advanced Battalion HQ in Rémeling with the words that he was holding on to his HQ with just twengty-eight men and had had no news of the other men in his company. The reaction from Advanced Battalion HQ was rapid and Second Lieutenant 'Ginger' Gall was dispatched with a fighting platoon to make contact with D Company. Private Tom Anderson was a member of that platoon:

> We had all been out the previous night on patrol and were sitting on the steps of the farmhouse when Gall came back and said, 'Right lads, I've just had a message that we're to go back out because we've lost contact with D Company. We're to find out what's happened. I'm looking for volunteers.' We all had our heads over our porridge and kept them there. I always remember what he said then, 'Oh if that's the way you feel about it, we'll all go back out'. We didn't normally go out in daylight so we had to crawl a good way up a ditch until we got into the cover of the wood. When we arrived at Company HQ, a lot of Germans were around but they soon cleared off.

There was some initial reluctance on the part of the men of Gall's platoon to go out again but eventually they arrived at the D Company Headquarters. On arrival at Company Gall was briefed by Lawrie and was asked to patrol up to the forward posts of the missing platoons and find out what happened. It was too late for many of the men as they had been overwhelmed by the weight of the German assault. The battle for Heydwald Wood had in fact severely damaged D Company: two officers and over sixty men were missing and six were wounded.

By 15 May it had become clear that the forward posts of the Division were unable to hold their own against increasing German assaults and General Fortune, in consultation with General Charles-Marie Condé, commanding the French Third Army, ordered a withdrawal to the *Ligne de Recueil* to match the French withdrawal. It was hardly a secure location:

> It lay about 3 miles in front of the Maginot line, on a forward slope. The field of fire was not good, the wire was thin, communication trenches were poor and an anti-tank ditch had only been half-dug. The Germans, however, did not press their advance. Extensive demolitions had been prepared along the Divisional Front and beside every charge two Sappers had waited patiently for the blessed order to blow. It came – and roads went skyward, bridges collapsed and trees tumbled. The German advance was usefully impeded, they came no further than the Obsterwald.

On 17 May the French division occupying the sector to the south of the Highlanders was withdrawn to prop up the Allied armies attempting to stem the German advance in the north and 154 Brigade were ordered by Général Condé to take over part of the vacated area – this probably sounded alarm bells in General Fortune's mind but there is no evidence that it did so.

On 20 May the bulk of the 51st Division was put into reserve under the direct control of the French Grand Quartier Général (CQG) and later had orders to move to the concentration area of Étain, about 20 miles west of Metz.

The move north

This was the first stage of the Division's return to the BEF, fighting further north; however, as they set off on their long journey, they had little or no knowledge of the German 2nd Panzer Division having reached the sea at Noyelles sur Mer and thereby preventing their movement to rejoin the BEF. No one knew what the plan for the Highlanders was although, as is usual in a crisis, countless rumours were in circulation. Six of the infantry battalions were to travel by train, the remainder of the Division by road. The destination for both groups was Pacy, 40 miles north-west of Paris, but as the strategic situation became clearer the 51st Division was shunted mercilessly from pillar to post in an effort to outrun the German advance. There was a great deal of confusion as orders were changed almost daily, so much so that officers and men were not absolutely sure where and when they would eventually arrive at their destination – wherever that was!

The Road Party

Heading for Gisors, the route took this group in a wide loop around the north of Paris. Moving a division across France was rather like moving a medium sized village, as Eric Linklater wrote in *The Highland Division*:

> The divisional Transport and lorry borne troops travelled about 300 miles on French roads. The movement of soldiers is never a simple operation and the Fifty First's march to the sea was made against time, in a country stupefied by sudden invasion, over roads that were roughly parallel to the German corridor and no more than 30-odd miles away from it. From the Forêt d'Argonne, where men, wagons and guns had lain hidden among the trees, to the Haute Forêt d'Eu, where they assembled for battle, was a three day journey in drill order; over an indicated route, at an ordered speed, in a fixed density of so many vehicles to the mile. Supply points and staging areas had to be arranged, advanced parties had to be told off, road pickets detailed, motor cyclists sent forward at such-and-such a time. The huge assortment of vehicles – there were about 3,000 of one sort or another – had to be marshalled according to their kind: Bren gun carriers and troop carriers, company vehicles and cooking trucks, blanket lorries in the transport echelon, water trucks, utility trucks and trucks mounting light machine guns for anti-aircraft defence. Despite the number the movement was completed speedily and without appreciable loss. Some idea of the problem of fuel supply may appear in the fact that

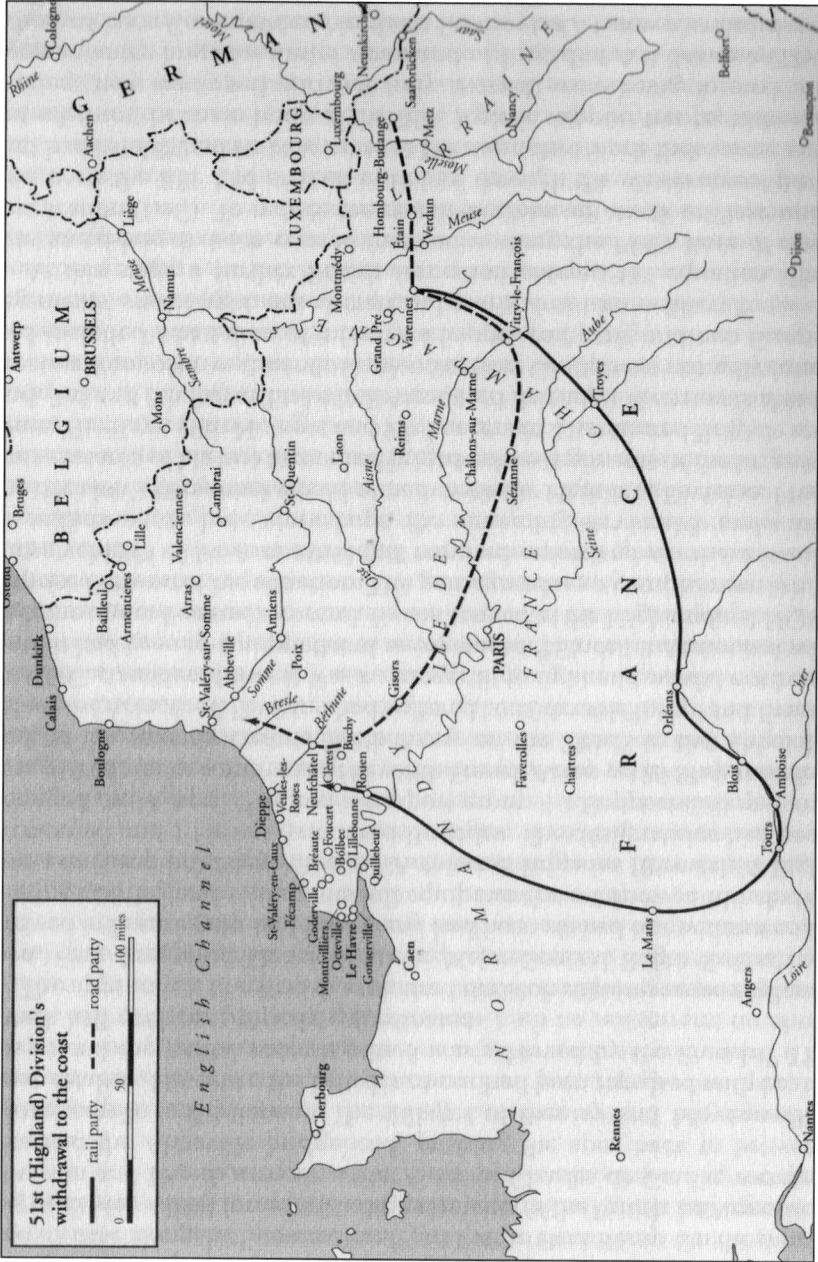

The two routes taken by the 51st Division when leaving the Saar region.

during the final month of its existence the division's average petrol consumption was 16,000 gallons per day.

As far as the north of Paris the roads were almost empty but from that point in the journey they met the inevitable streams of refugee traffic, all doing their best to escape from the invaders further north. Not only that, but the clouds of dust that were thrown up by the convoy managed to inflame the eyes of the drivers and dispatch riders to an alarming degree. Nevertheless there were very few who did not make it to the battlefields of Normandy.

The Train Party

The train party took a long route around the south of Paris, via Vitry le Francois, where apparently the train stopped in a station as a French ammunition train had been hit by an air raid about ten minutes before and was busy exploding. When the ammunition had all gone off the troop train containing the rail party continued on its way. At one point the six battalions that travelled by train had 'vanished' without the Division being informed of their whereabouts; it seems they had been redirected along the Loire valley to Rouen and Le Mans by a rather panicky French command. The train eventually stopped near Neufchâtel, where they took to the roads of Normandy in French buses. Although the buses took them at a furious pace along roads of dubious quality, at least they were sheltered from marauding German bombers by a heavy mist and pouring rain. The whole column was directed by a French subaltern armed with a megaphone in a small Citroen. Miraculously, during the 60 or so miles of the journey, there were no casualties.

A railway truck typical of those in which the 51st Division were transported from the Saar to the Somme.

Chapter 4

The 1st Armoured Division
The attacks of 24 and 27 May

When considering the plight of the 51st Division it would be worthwhile taking some time to consider the overall strategic situation. It has already been explained that the 1st Armoured Division was not technically a part of the 51st Division but, as it worked closely with the Highlanders and fell under the command of the French Général Robert Altmayer, it has been included in this account.

Initial elements of the 1st Armoured Division landed at Le Havre on 15 May and advanced parties had reached Arras, where it was intended to concentrate the Division. However, the approach of the German Panzers and enemy bombing made it clear this would be impossible. Accordingly, Major General Roger Evans, the commander of the Armoured Division, arranged for the remainder of it to be landed at Cherbourg, with the training area at Pacy-sur-Eure. Although it was fast becoming clear that the BEF was now being cut off from the French forces in the south, Gort still firmly believed that the gap in Général André-Georges Corap's Ninth French Army must be closed if disaster was to be prevented. (The German

Général Robert Altmeyer (*left*) and Général André-Georges Corap (*right*).

39

Panzer divisions that had broken through at Sedan had created a large gap in Corap's sector.) But as Gort later explained to General Edmund Ironside, who was Chief of the Imperial General Staff at the time, this was an undertaking that the French had to initiate from the south. From the relative security of the Cabinet Office in London such a plan seemed very sensible, the 5th and 50th Divisions were earmarked to support any Allied attempt to attack towards Amiens and Gort remained faithful in supporting Général Alphonse Georges assertion that the Third Army Group, under the command of Général Antoine-Marie-Benoit Besson, was being assembled in the south. Gort may well have remained sceptical about the success of the plan but it would appear that the Frank Force tank attack at Arras of 21 May was planned with a view to advancing alongside the

Général Antoine-Marie-Benoît Besson.

French in order to cut off the German lines of communications. All of this rather negates the theory that the Arras counterstroke was designed as a stand-alone offensive. Général Maxime Weygand possibly even entertained thoughts that the 1st Armoured Division, along with the 51st Division, would work together to link up with the increasingly beleaguered

Général Maxime Weygand.

BEF, but first the 51st Division had to complete its slow and tortuous journey from the Saar!

Barely two weeks into the German assault of 10 May, the situation was looking extremely bad for Britain and France and plans were being discussed for the withdrawal of the BEF back to England. However, despite this, the British government was continuing to send units to France in the vain hope of restoring the situation and halting the rapid German advance. One of these formations was the 1st Armoured Division. Although the 1st Armoured Division was a separate division from the 51st Division, the two formations worked closely with one another. Needless to say it was hardly a force to be reckoned with. The 2nd (Light) Armoured Brigade, for example, consisted of 257 tanks, mainly Mark VIB and VIC tanks, although there were some A13 Cruiser tanks but which were only present in small numbers. There was a distinct lack of basic equipment in the brigade, such as armour piercing ammunition and wireless sets. Not only that but the new BESA machine guns were yet to be unpacked and the crews had little or no training on these weapons. One 9/Lancers Cruiser tank actually went to France without its gun, such was the desperate shortage, the intention being to cannibalize the first tank that was knocked out. One observer even went so far as to say that, 'the 1st Armoured Division was completely emasculated from the onset and deprived of any striking power'. It should be noted that the divisional infantry, 2/Kings Royal Rifle Brigade, the 1/ Rifle Brigade, and the 3/Royal Tank Regiment, had been sent to Calais in a futile attempt to save the city, and all of these were killed or captured when Calais fell on 26 May. Thus the Division was by no means complete when it disembarked at Cherbourg.

The 2nd (Light) Armoured Brigade included the 2nd Dragoon Guards (Queens Bays), the 9th Queen's Royal Lancers and the 10th Royal Hussars (Prince of Wales Own). The 10/Royal Hussars was commanded by Lieutenant Colonel John Hignett, the Bays by Lieutenant Colonel George Draffen and the 9/Lancers by Lieutenant Colonel Christopher Peto. The first elements of the 1st Armoured Division were placed on stand-by in France on 13 May, ostensibly to move to Pacy-sur-Eure, but by 16 May the Division was warned for immediate action and the orders for Pacy were cancelled. There then followed a period of confusion as the rapidly developing situation overtook the Division before it was finally decided, after all, to concentrate at Pacy-sur-Eure. On 21 May Amiens was captured by the Germans and two days later the 51st Division completed its concentration in the Étain area.

It was only later, on 25 May, that Fortune's staff was informed that the six battalions travelling by train had been re-routed to Rouen! Fortune was incensed and he insisted to Général Besson that the division be allowed to concentrate properly before being committed to an operational role. It was agreed on 26 May that both the road and rail parties would concentrate

Lieutenant Colonel John Hignett commanded the 10/Royal Hussars.

between the Rivers Bresle and Béthune before moving forward to the Somme and take up the line from the sea to Pont-Remy.

Meanwhile, on 23 May, the 2nd (Light) Armoured Brigade was visited by a general staff officer, Lieutenant Colonel Raymond Briggs, who had orders to send a maximum force at once to force crossings over the Somme and advance on St-Pol. This was an ambitious task for a division without infantry, field guns or air support! Nevertheless, on 23 May, Brigadier Richard McCreery, commanding the 2nd (Light) Armoured Brigade, advanced towards the Somme with a small support group that included the 4/Border Regiment (from the Beauman Division).

Lieutenant Colonel Raymond Briggs arrived with orders to take the Somme crossings.

On 23 May the 4/Battalion was ordered to move forward and report to the commander of the 2nd Armoured Brigade, which was then a few miles south of the Somme, just west of Amiens. Arriving in the early hours of 24 May, the battalion was ordered to attack, supported by one regiment of tanks, the three bridges over the Somme at Saveuse, Ailly and Picquigny.

The Bays made contact with the enemy on the south bank of the Somme between Longpré and Pont-Remy and found all the Bridges mined or blown. The 4/Border Regiment then launched C Company over the damaged bridge at Ailly (each bridge was to be accompanied by a troop of tanks from the Bays) but this party, without any artillery support, made no progress and incurred heavy losses. D Company then advanced from the woods south of Picquigny.

This attack illustrated in a nutshell most of the shortfalls that were to dog the British armoured divisions over the next few years. Lieutenant Gavin and his I Troop of tanks fortunately approached the bridge on a different road to D Company, the company meanwhile running headlong into an ambush whilst Gavin gave covering fire where he could. Unfortunately, Captain Leslie Richmond was killed while trying to cross the bridge. (He is commemorated on the Dunkerque Memorial.) The fighting continued for much of the day, with about fifteen men of the Borderers reaching the tank lines where French ambulances were waiting. The Bays lost six tanks from enemy action and five men killed, four wounded and six missing.

A Company attacked Saveuse with two light tanks. After capturing the village they met with severe opposition from enemy machine guns and failed to reach the bridge. It was, to put it bluntly, an incursion that was

Men of the 4/Borderers moving towards the Somme, 23 May 1940.

bound to fail; eventually the three companies arrived back at Battalion HQ at the Fôret d'Helle. As for the Bays, they were relieved by the 10/Hussars and the 9/Lancers, who withdrew to a wood while the Border Regiment held a skirmishing line near to the scene of the action.

On 25 May orders were received from Général Weygand that the 1st Armoured Division would work with Robert Altmeyer's group, which included the 2nd and 5th Light Mechanized Divisions (DLM), in establishing bridgeheads over the Somme. The British 2nd Armoured Brigade was to support the 2nd DLM, while the 3rd Armoured Brigade was to support the 5th DLM by advancing on the south bank of the Somme from Longpré-les-Corps-Saints.

The next day, the 26 May, while moves to conform with this plan were being made and the condition of the British Armoured Division was being explained to the French commanders, so that the latter should be under no illusion as to our equipment, the British Government gave orders for the encircled BEF to start embarkation for England at Dunkirk.

In fact General Evans had been called to the Headquarters of Général Altmayer and informed a major attack was scheduled to take place the

A vehicle of the (French) 5th Light Mechanized Division.

following day with the purpose of driving in the enemy bridgehead at Abbeville. His formation was expected to pave the way for the two French divisions and, on explaining his tanks were totally unsuited for this sort of work, Altmayer would have none of it. He told Evans that those were his orders and it was up to him to carry them out. Thus, on the very day the Belgians capitulated, the 2nd Armoured Brigade were given orders to attack the bridgehead covering the Somme crossings at Abbeville and link up with the BEF.

The line of attack saw the Bays on the right and the 10/Hussars on the left, with the final objective given as Pont Remy-Les Planches. French reports stated this area was lightly held by inferior troops equipped with light anti-tank weapons, a report that was later to be found incorrect: the position was strongly held by elements of IR 25, armed with 3.7 PAK anti-tank guns.

To the British, cut off in the north, it must have appeared imperative to force the crossings of the Somme to allow an immediate advance towards St-Pol to cut across the rear of the Germans and relieve the threat to the right of the BEF. However, with the 1st Armoured Division not yet concentrated, as well as the infantry support group and a regiment of tanks sent to Calais, it was not able fully to comply. Nevertheless, orders were orders and instructions were issued for the move.

The Attack of 27 May

General Evans was informed that the advance would begin at 5.00am on 27 May along a sector stretching from Abbeville to St Valery-sur-Somme. The 3rd Armoured Brigade were to secure St Valery-sur-Somme while the 2nd Armoured Brigade were to clear the roads to Abbeville and break through German lines along the line of the villages of Bailleul, Limeux and Huppy. The 2nd Armoured Brigade was under the orders of Colonel André Berniquet, commanding the French 2/Light Cavalry Division; and the 3/Armoured Brigade was under the orders of General Marie-Jacques-Henri Chanoine, commanding the French 5/Light Cavalry Division. Within the 2nd Armoured Brigade boundary, the Bays would assault Bailleul and the 10/Hussars would focus on Huppy. The 9/Lancers would be in reserve with Brigade HQ at Oisemont. The 10/Hussars began their move on the holding area at about 2.00am on the morning of 26 May, with A Squadron and Regimental HQ at Ramburelles, B Squadron at Framicourt and C Squadron at Biencourt. Sgt Ron Huggins describes A Squadron's arrival at their holding area:

> We arrived at Ramburelles at about 0730 on 26 May. Our tanks were dispersed around the small village green and under the boundary wall of a large country house, where we camouflaged them with tree branches and other greenery. Guard tanks were positioned on the approach roads leading northwards and eastwards out of the village in case of a surprise attack.

The start line for the attack carried out by the 10/Hussars on the left was the railway line that ran between Oisemont and St Maxent, with the attack due to go off at 0500 on 27 May. There was also the promise of French infantry and a battery of French 75-mm guns to fire on Huppy between 5.10 and 5.30am; however, the attack was put back by about an hour as the French gunners were not ready.

By a cruel coincidence the dispatch rider sent to the 10/Hussars was killed on his way to Ramburelles and the Regiment never received the message. Even so, there had been no time allowed for a careful reconnaissance and only vague information about German strength was available. This was just as well, as the German positions were well dug in and forward of Abbeville in the villages of Moyenneville, Huppy and Caumont, and they had a number of anti-tank guns hidden in the woods. Against such well prepared positions the tanks could have had little effect and, to cap it all, the co-operation with the French was ineffective and close support was almost non-existent. This was hardly a recipe for success.

The 10/Hussars, on the left wing of the 2/Armoured Brigade, advanced into a maelstrom of fire from the guns of 14/Kompanie:

> The anti-tank Kompanie of IR25 was emplaced in the south end of the village of Huppy. The town had only one approach route. The men

knew that, and as the spear head of the XXXVIII Armee Korps on the left margin of the Somme, they set up a hastily organized position. It was at dawn when, shortly after 0500, the sound of heavy motors were heard. They could not be trucks so they must be tanks. Alarm! And the hunters occupied their positions behind their arms (guns). At about 0530 we detected the first enemy tanks advancing on German positions.

C Squadron of the 10/Hussars immediately took several casualties, the armour of the light tanks of the squadron easily penetrated by the 3.7-mm anti-tank guns operated by 14 Kompanie. Schütze Hubert Brinkforth worked furiously at his gun, loading, aiming and firing at the oncoming tanks. The official German report of the battle singles Brinkforth out for specific mention:

> The Anti-Tank position had identified its targets. At 0542 Brinkforth saw his first tank, the loader prepared an anti-tank grenade. Brinkforth tried to count how many enemies were coming at them. About fifteen tanks, he stopped counting. Then came the order from the gun leader, Unteroffizer Krohn: 'Open Fire!' The grenade fired by Brinkforth hit the first British tank at 150 metres. First there was no effect, then the tank was slowly stopping and then suddenly came a flash from the tower and a loud explosion, the enemy tank blew though the air.

Brinkforth accounted for eleven of the 10/Hussar's tanks and was awarded the German Knight's Cross. He was killed in June 1942 on the Russian Front. The British attack was a failure, the 10/Hussars losing four officers, including Captain Wyndham Malet, and fourteen other ranks and two officers wounded, as well as thirty tanks lost during the battle. (Captain Wyndham Malet is buried in Ramburelles Churchyard Cemetery.)

On McCreery's right flank the Queen's Bays were unaware of the 10/Hussars' debacle and pressed on towards Bailleul. Near the Bois de Limeux they ran into another German anti-tank position and four tanks were destroyed in the Bay's lead squadron. A deluge of fire from machine guns, mortars and infantry guns was directed at the Bays, keeping them contained, at which point the tanks'

Schütze Hubert Brinkforth.

A map taken from the 1990 edition of *The Journal of the Royal Hussars* drawn by Sergeant Ron Huggins, showing his movements around Huppy on 27 May 1940.

radios chose to malfunction and the close support tanks, which were intended to mask the enemy anti-tank guns with smoke, ran out of ammunition. A few Cruiser Mark IIIs made it past the German outpost line and possibly reached Huchenneville before they were knocked out; after losing twelve tanks, the Bays withdrew.

On the left wing, the 3/Armoured Brigade found less opposition outside the Abbeville bridgehead and reached the high ground overlooking the

49

A VIC Tank knocked out at Huppy.

Two British tanks at Huppy; the state of the vehicles is not known.

The lone CWGC headstone marks the grave of Captain Wyndham Malet at Ramburelles Churchyard.

Somme near Cambron and Saigneville and the outskirts of St Valery-sur-Somme at the river mouth. However, with no supporting troops the British tanks were withdrawn, nothing of any particular value had been achieved and the German hold on their bridgehead has not been disturbed. Using Cruiser tanks unsupported by artillery and infantry had incurred heavy losses, sixty-five tanks had been put out of action and some fifty-five had mechanical breakdowns. Only light repairs on the battlefield were possible whilst the divisional workshops, where major repairs were carried out, were south-west of Rouen. Altogether a lesson was learned in how not to attack a well entrenched enemy! That evening the 2/Armoured Brigade had withdrawn, leaving the 9/Lancers at Ramburelles in support of the French. The 3/Armoured Brigade withdrew to the area of Feuquières. The 1st Armoured Division lost 120 out of the 180 tanks engaged. McCreery's 2/Armoured Brigade was eventually withdrawn to Rouen, while the 3/Armoured Brigade remained as a mobile reserve.

The next day, on 28 May, the French attacked again and although some divisions reached the Somme they could not loosen the enemy's hold on Abbeville and St Valery-sur-Somme. De Gaulle's (French) 4th Armoured Division attacked the next day astride the Blangy-Abbeville road but was stopped by well placed anti-tank defences in the woods and on the ridge running north-west from Villers-sur-Mareuil. Once again it had little or no artillery support and without any infantry to consolidate the ground won, there was little gained. He attacked again on 30 May, supported by elements of the remaining French divisions (the 2nd and 5th Light Cavalry) and the British troops held in reserve. The attack, once again, failed to dislodge the enemy and so at the end of four days of fighting the enemy's bridgeheads on the Somme remained untaken.

There our story of the 1st Armoured Division effectively ends as we continue with the demise of the 51st Division as it wound its way through Normandy to St Valery-en-Caux. The 1st Armoured Division continued in action, albeit split into composite forces, until it was evacuated.

Huppy and Moyennville were eventually taken by De Gaulle's force, albeit temporarily; the German guns on Mount Caumont remained intact and Weygand turned the Abbeville sector over to the 51st Division, which was finally reassembled after its journey from the Saar. It is said that on

Général Charles de Gaulle reviewing French troops.

the opposite side of the Somme, Kluge's Fourth Army was pressed to conduct a counter-attack using the 2nd Infantry Division and the 9th Panzer Division but Kluge refused, wanting his mobile divisions well rested before *Fall Rot*. Whether this is true or not remains hidden in the murk of unrecorded history.

James Marshall-Cornwall and Henry Karslake

Behind the scenes, Lieutenant General Sir James Marshall-Cornwall was appointed to head the new No. 17 Military Mission, attached to the French Tenth Army, in order to 'watch over' the interests of the British 1st Armoured and the 51st (Highland) divisions. They were the only British fighting formations that remained under Weygand's control and Marshall-Cornwall's instructions were to attach himself to the French Army Headquarters under which these formations were placed.

There was a degree of controversy about this appointment, in that Lieutenant General Sir Edmund Ironside, the CIGS at the time, subsequently ordered Lieutenant General Henry Karslake on 23 May to Le Mans as a corps commander to take over the control of the 120,000 British troops on the Lines of Communications. His appointment would be confirmed later.

However, on 27 May Ironside was replaced as CIGS by Sir John Dill and Karslake's appointment was never confirmed in writing, leaving both generals in limbo. Karslake remained in position as commander of the Lines of Communication troops but with no operational control over any other unit than Beauman's, which was essentially seen as a base force and

Lieutenant General Sir James Marshall-Cornwall.

53

A conference at Neuborg on 9 June 1940. From left to right: Major Fanshaw ADC, ANO, Lieutenant General Sir James Marshall-Cornwall, Lieutenant General Sir Henry Karslake and Major General Evans.

not equipped for active service. But there was no British overall commander. Typical of the occasions when the absence of an overall commander was felt can be found in Altmayer's unreasonable request on 26 May. Altmayer ordered that the tanks of 1st Armoured Division were to be used against prepared enemy positions. Evans explained that his tanks bore little resemblance to the heavy tanks of the French and were more suited to employment against ground troops in the open. But General Evans had no one to whom he could appeal, his division was not under Karslake and Altmayer was adamant that Evans should do as he was told; the outcome is described above.

When Sir Alan Brooke arrived at Le Mans on 13 June to take command of the Second BEF he apparently realized Karslake was the 'fifth wheel of the coach' and sent him straight back to England. There were several who were pleased to see him go, particularly as he had upset the *status quo* on several occasions; in the meantime there had been two senior officers at large, neither of whom had much jurisdiction over the British 51st and the 1st Armoured divisions. It was, to put it bluntly, a typical British mess for which no one would take the blame.

General Fortune soon realized that Marshall-Cornwall's role was one of observation; he could only pass on the orders of Tenth Army Headquarters but had no influence over them. At the same time the various British formation commanders were overwhelmed by a massive French hierarchy.

54

Basil Karslake, the son of Henry Karslake, wrote in *The Last Act* that the British units, south of the Somme, were constrained by the command situation that they found themselves in:

> They owed allegiance to all and sundry from whom they could receive orders at any time, all quite independent of one another. In addition it was quite possible for them to receive orders from the War Office in London; these could be at variance with those received from their French commanders. In this latter connection, it should be pointed out that French orders had priority. Also there was no appeal against them. No overall [British] commander had been appointed. It is difficult to believe that the reader will be able to disentangle this situation any more than the British then in France.

Righly or wrongly, Karslake, who had been restored to the active list after he retired in 1938, left France on 13 June on the orders of Sir Alan Brooke and died on 19 October 1942. James Marshall-Cornwall remained in 'post', was evacuated from France on the SS *Manxman*, boarding the last ship to leave Cherbourg; he took up several widely different appointments in the army, retiring in 1943. He died on 25 December 1985.

Chapter 5

Retreat from the Somme

After the attack on Abbeville, the 51st Division's battlefield was defined by the Rivers Somme, Bresle and Béthune and began with a withdrawal that would end with the last stand at St Valery-en-Caux. While the abortive attempts were being made to recover the Somme crossings, the BEF in the north withdrew into a bridgehead at Dunkirk and was in the process of being evacuated to England. The 51st Division had been arriving in the Bresle area from the Saar front, moving into their Divisional HQ at St Leger, south of Blangy, on 28 May.

Despite the obvious fact that after 25 May there was little hope of a link-up between the Allied forces in the north and the south of the Somme, Weygand still demanded that the German bridgeheads should be eliminated. One has to wonder why the Germans were not immediately prevented from crossing the Somme, given the numbers of men and quantity of *materiel* that the Allies had, but since Sedan perhaps the French had already given thoughts of surrender too much credence. Despite unsuccessful French and British efforts to eliminate the Abbeville bridgehead with a consequent high casualty rate, Weygand reckoned one more push, with fresh units, would drive the Germans off Mont de Caumont and open the way north.

In many ways this thinking was reminiscent of that of Haig during the Ypres offensive of 1917 during the First World War. Certainly allowing the counter-offensive to be planned by a British infantry commander, in which the main strike force was to be a French armoured division, raised eyebrows and pointed towards French military minds being fuzzy, to say the least. Surely the best placed to produce the plan were French officers who were more knowledgeable about the enemy and terrain than Fortune's staff? To cap it all, Fortune's staff were barely able to communicate with the

Général Maxime Weygand.

French units they were supposed to liaise with owing to a lack of trained officers who spoke French (or, conversely, English). Even to the casual observer it must have appeared obvious that the attack was doomed to failure even before it was conceived.

The River Somme at Abbeville.

The basic concept was to attack the enemy bridgehead from three directions: from the west, south and south-east. Both of the Allied infantry divisions would only contribute three of their battalions each, which 152 Brigade was selected to provide on the British side. The intention was that the 51st Division, along with the French 31st Division, would attack and capture the Abbeville bridgehead; while the general objective of the attack was to secure the high ground on the south west bank of the Somme and to dominate the Somme crossings.

58

At 3.30am on Tuesday 4 June the Allied counter-attack began with an opening artillery barrage on the German positions on Mont de Caumont. As the Germans were well dug in and thus consequently to a great extent shielded from the artillery, the barrage was largely ineffective. What Allied intelligence had not bothered to pass on (or were perhaps still in the dark about) was that *Fall Rot* was due to begin the next day and therefore a large number of German troops were present in the Abbeville bridgehead.

The attack by the British and French was to be carried out in four distinct phases: A particularly brilliant incident of the day was the highly successful attack by the 1/Gordons against enemy forces entrenched in the Grand Bois. The 1/Gordons, supported by the 1/Kensingtons and one troop from 53/Anti-Tank Regiment, were to capture the spur overlooking Cambron. Second Lieutenant 'Reg' Wood was fighting with the 1/Kensingtons and recorded the results of the artillery bombardment and subsequent advance in his diary:

> At 3.00am a terrific artillery bombardment of the two woods began, shell after shell went whistling over, landing with a terrific roar amidst dust, smoke and debris in the woods. For half an hour this crashing cascade of shells went over and it seemed impossible that anything could be left alive in the woods. At 3.30am a Very Light went up on our left and the Gordons started their attack through the wood. Soon another light went up, which meant we were to put down suppressing fire just in front of them as they advanced ... A red light went up and then we stopped firing. After an interval of ten minutes a hail of machine gun bullets came whizzing over. We were directly exposed and I never felt so uncomfortable in all my life, with only long grass in front of us and no protection at all. A corporal who was lying beside me was hit in the shoulder and an

Second Lieutenant 'Reg' B.R. Wood, 4 Platoon commander, 1/Kensingtons.

> OR (other rank), whose arm was touching mine, was hit by a bullet and shot in the head ... It was obvious something has gone wrong with the attack as they should have crossed the gap to attack the Bois de Cambron. [The gap was between the two woods, the Grand Bois and the Bois de Cambron.]

Something had indeed gone wrong. The French tanks had run out of petrol a mile from their objective, causing the 4/Seaforths to advance across open country, which was swept by murderous machine gun and mortar fire. The

1/Gordons had consequently stopped when they got to the end of the Grand Bois and were consolidating their positions.

Phase two was an attack by the French and 2/Armoured Brigade on the Somme Canal west of Abbeville and phase three was an attack by the French 2nd Armoured Division on the twin ridges overlooking Abbeville, the Mont de Caubert spur and another ridge of high ground. This was in effect the crux of the whole attack and was supported by the 4/Seaforths, D Company of the 1/Kensingtons and the 51/Anti-Tank Regiment.

Phase four was an attack by the 4/Camerons, supported by another company of the 1/Kensingtons, on Caubert and a nearby wood. Only one officer and forty other ranks of the company survived this attack; the Kensington war diary records the withering machine gun fire met by the 4/Camerons:

> Due to bitter hand to hand fighting it was not easy for the Kensingtons to lay down effective counter fire without hitting the Camerons, but whenever the opportunity occurred the Germans were given a great deal of their own medicine and this undoubtedly helped lessen the severe casualties sustained. On the left another company of the Camerons, supported by a further machine gun section and French tanks, proceeded to attack Caubert and succeeded, after fierce engagements, in reaching the first objective, only to be met as they advanced, by intense machine gun fire from a ridge dominating the countryside, which was supposed to have been captured by French tanks.

The attack failed. On Mont Caumont French tanks first encountered the mines that had been previously laid by the Germans (which had been unaccountably missed by Allied planners) and reached the top, where they overran some trenches before the Luftwaffe 88s saved the Germans' day. Only three tanks that ascended Mont Caumont returned to French lines: about forty tanks were destroyed. The British 152 Brigade had achieved very little. Altogether Stewart's Brigade suffered 563 casualties and several companies were virtually destroyed. By the afternoon of 4 June it was obvious that Weygand's bid to overcome the Abbeville bridgehead had failed, mainly because of the German's greater strength and cohesiveness and the insufficient time given for preparation. Allied troops had made several attempts against the bridgehead but had ultimately been driven back each time.

Summary

This is probably a good occasion to review the position in which the 51st Division now found itself. As we know, the Germans had reached the Channel coast on 20 May and by so doing had cut the Division off from the main body of the BEF. There were now 140,000 British troops south of the Somme; many of these were Lines of Communication troops and men of the base garrison. To the north the Dunkirk evacuation concluded

Only three tanks that ascended Mont Caumont returned to French lines; about forty tanks were destroyed by German 88mm guns.

on 4 June with a total of over 330,000 Allied troops landed in England. The attack on 4 June by the 51st Division and French units on the Abbeville bridgehead had failed and the German counter-attack (*Fall Rot*) of 5 June had inflicted heavy casualties on the Division and consequently left it severely weakened. General Fortune secured an agreement (it should be noted that this was given reluctantly) from Général Altmayer for the Division to move back to the River Bresle, some 12 miles to the south.

The 7 and 8/Argyll and Sutherland Highlanders
Fall Rot had begun in the early hours of 5 June; the 11/Motorized Brigade and 12th Infantry Division were pitted against the British south of the Somme valley, namely the two forward battalions, both of the Argyll and Sutherland Highlanders, of 154 Brigade. They were facing the German bridgehead at Valery-sur-Somme from Saigneville to the sea.

Prior to the attack the 7/Argylls were on the right flank, with Battalion HQ at Franleu, B Company was at Saigneville, C Company held Mons-Boubert in the centre while D Company held Cattigny and Arrest on the left. A Company was initially holding Guoy and Cahon but was moved to a reserve position at Quesnoy-le-Montant. On 1 June Private William Sutherland was killed with A Company during a skirmish with enemy

61

A map showing the dispositions of the 7/Argyll and Sutherland Highlanders on 5 June 1940.

Fall Rot, the German offensive, began on 5 June 1940.

patrols, an abrupt sign of things to come? (28-year-old Sutherland is remembered on the Dunkirk Memorial.)

The 8/Argylls were nearest the sea, on the left, with their Battalion HQ at St Blimont and the remaining three companies in the villages of Sallenelle, Lancheres and Pende. The only means of contact between the village outposts and their respective company headquarters was by telephone line, which laid itself open to being easily cut.

Just after daylight Second Lieutenant Moore of the 7/Argylls was in position on the forward edge of the Bois de Nevers, in front of the D and C Company positions at Catigny and Mons-Boubert, when he heard shouts from his sections posts. Running back to the posts he met a runner who reported large numbers of Germans advancing from the wood. Giving instructions not to open fire until the enemy were in range, he ran back to Headquarters to collect a Very pistol in case a request for artillery assistance was necessary. At about the same time mortar shells began landing and Moore sent a dispatch rider to Battalion Headquarters to warn them of the situation and a signal to 17/Field Regiment requesting an artillery bombardment. No artillery salvo ever arrived, as 17/Field Regiment was fighting a battle of its own.

At about 4.10am Private Malone arrived at Franleu on his motorbike and lost little time in locating the Commanding Officer in the schoolhouse that was serving as Battalion Headquarters. Edmund Buchanan immediately ordered a troop of four carriers under Second Lieutenant Robert Powell to move *post-haste* to Mons-Boubert and report to the C Company commander, Captain Hewitt, in a bid to prevent the enemy from cutting off C Company from Franleu. At the same time he placed an artillery officer in the church tower. Meanwhile Moore was unaware of the attempt by the carriers to clear a passage between him and the village and had gone back to his section, who were firing furiously from the front of the wood. Moore gave the order for the centre section to withdraw, as their ammunition had all but expired, and then almost pushed them into the standing corn. No similar order reached the other sections. Moore felt the whole response to the enemy was a little disorganized:

> My intention here was to rally the other sections, who were rather disorganized by this time owing to the heavy enemy mortaring. Shortly after my arrival at this junction, one single enemy appeared a short distance to the right and doubled across the road. I fired at him. He returned my fire. A second German now appeared from the place where the last one had come from and fired at me. He missed, and I returned his fire. He fell. I was then hit in the left arm. I swung round to fire again at the first German. He was aiming at me with his rifle. I took a deliberate aim with my revolver. We appeared to fire at the same time. I fell wounded in the thigh. He appeared to let out a groan and fell backwards.

Moore was captured at about 5.30am and the remaining British soldiers were mopped up. In the intervening time Lieutenant Powell had taken up a position on the south west of C Company at Mons-Boubert, where his carriers went into action and immediately engaged the enemy at 200 yards range. As a result of this his carriers inflicted a large number of casualties. Eventually the enemy brought up anti-tank guns and after one carrier was knocked out the remainder withdrew into the village, where they were used to strengthen C Company's defences.

During this time the Battalion HQ was fighting its own battle as the enemy advanced close up to Franleu and were engaging posts on the forward edge of the village. Soon the Germans advanced into the village itself and came to within 50 yards of Battalion Headquarters; it became obvious that the men inside the schoolhouse could not hope to hold the position unaided for much longer and A Company from Quesnoy was ordered back to assist.

The CO, 41-year-old Captain Glenn Handley, and the reserve platoon under Lieutenant Haig were the first to arrive but their truck received a direct hit as they entered the village. Handley was mortally wounded and Haig continued to the orchard in front of the schoolhouse, where he took up a defensive position. (Handley is buried at St Riquier British Cemetery, near Abbeville.) By this time two patrols had been organized by RSM

The Schoolhouse at Franleu: view from the playground.

Lockie and CSM Dyer and the enemy were cleared from the vicinity of the orchard. Sometime later the remainder of A Company reached the village and took up positions on the east and west side of Battalion Headquarters at Franleu.

At about 6.00am B Company reported the enemy were advancing up to their positions but were being successfully kept under fire by the Kensingtons. In addition, the enemy was observed to be massing in a ravine about

1,000 yards west of Saignville , An artillery barrage, requested by the Company Commander, Captain John Logan, proved highly successful in dispersing the attackers. Unfortunately, because the enemy could advance between the company strong points and overrun the unprotected artillery, such success was rare and later, when Logan requested a further shoot, he was informed the artillery had withdrawn. About this time two soldiers from the 54/Light Anti-Aircraft Regiment came into the battalion lines. They had escaped from Boulogne and remained behind enemy lines for ten days until they swam the River Somme to relative safety. There is no mention of them afterwards, so it is assumed they were captured at St Valery-en-Caux.

The last message to brigade was passed at about 9.00am, after which the wireless truck was blown up and the battalion was left to fight on alone. The Commanding Officer, however, had a hard enough task to defend Franleu, as all day long the enemy kept up a relentless pressure. One attack after another was repulsed and through all of this a persistent shower of mortar bombs added misery to the defenders. It should be noted that the battalion's mortars were not inactive and they were constantly moving from one position to another until their ammunition ran out. But the Germans had the superior 5-cm mortars, which were by far more accurate. The enemy fire grew more intense but they still showed no inclination to come out into the open. From the church tower a mass of enemy soldiers and equipment could be seen passing to the west of the village, apparently unconcerned by the British soldiers defending Franleu.

As each company of the 7/Argylls was surrounded, and the number of casualties increased, the day wore on and, in the absence of the Medical Officer (MO), the battalion Padre, the Rev Duncan MacInnes, converted the cellars below the schoolhouse into a makeshift regimental aid post (ROP), which soon became full to capacity. The Commanding Officer, Edmund 'Copper' Buchanan, was mystified about the missing MO:

> I sent a runner to the ROP . . . to confirm this report or fetch the MO.
> The runner reported on his return that the ROP had been evacuated,
> and that there was no sign of the MO or his orderlies, or of the ambu-
> lance, MO's truck or medical pannier.

One can only assume that the MO had gone 'astray' from Franleu when it became evident that they were not going to get out of the village in one piece! The situation in the village soon became hopeless. A shell, which landed at the entrance to the schoolhouse, wounded the adjutant, the Headquarters Company Commander, Captain Alistair Robertson, and the intelligence officer; and by 4.00pm the only officers that remained un-wounded were Lieutenant Haig and the Commanding Officer.

While the Argylls were fighting for their lives, Brigadier Stanley-Clarke at Belloy was trying desperately to organize some relief. Eventually Stanley-Clarke managed to persuade General Fortune to release the

(*Left*) Captain John Logan. (*Right*) The Rev Duncan MacInnes in his robes as a bishop after the war.

4/Black Watch from reserve at Le Plouay. Together with a detachment of French tanks they arrived at Valines, one mile behind Franleu. This is as far as they got and no counter-attack was made. The reason given for this inaction by the Commanding Officer of the Black Watch was that, without the support of the French tanks, which were late arriving, it was suicide to advance across ground that had little or no cover. He may well have been

British troops manning a roadblock.

Men of the 7/Argylls a few days before *Fall Rot*.

right, but the decision cost the Franleu garrison any hope of rescue. To this day the 7/Argylls accuse the 4/Black Watch of leaving them to their fate.

The following day more and more enemy units kept moving forward on their flank and, although the survivors took a heavy toll of these men, it appeared that two platoons of British infantry were insufficient to warrant much attention. By the afternoon the enemy had decided to eliminate this thorn in their side and repeated attacks were made, each preceded by a heavy mortar attack but each time the attack was repulsed by the rapidly diminishing defenders. At about 4.30pm they surrendered. The last act of this gallant company was to destroy all of its weapons and Lieutenant Fisher was conducted to the German commander and congratulated on the fight they had put up. However, Second Lieutenant Haig made a break for freedom with about ten of his platoon and the battalion intelligence officer, who, despite his wounds, joined him in his bid for freedom:

> I was down in the cellar with the wounded men when, in the afternoon, the CO said, 'Well, those who think they have a chance of getting away can try.' My sergeant had managed to get the water truck, which had been hit earlier. Started up and got me out along with my batman. A water truck is a really big container with very little room for passengers; because of this, there were only eight of us, mostly of my section, on it. The sergeant drove but I knew the way because I had come up with the CO a few days earlier. We drove westwards and only stopped once to clear a barricade of carts and things from the road. Then, just as we came round a corner, there was a

68

German machine gun! They weren't expecting us and the gun wasn't manned. We went as fast as we could and as we passed by they hit one of our chaps who fell off, but we couldn't stop. Then we were away.

Another truck with wounded and Captain Forbes-Hendry, the mortar officer, also managed to escape, along with two Bren gun carriers. He was successful, possibly because most of the guns were facing in the opposite direction. Then it was the turn of 'Copper' Buchanan who, with the artillery spotter, Second Lieutenant Thomas and two NCOs, managed to get as far as open ground, where they were fired upon and pinned to the ground. Their bid for freedom had ended. On 7 June the effective strength of the battalion was five officers and 130 other ranks.

The German counter-attack was now driving the whole Division back, the front was too long and its defenders few in number. It was a physical and numerical impossibility to hold the line with only one division but, on the plus side, if one can refer to a plus side, nowhere was the line abandoned without serious fighting. The words 'impossible task' and 'overwhelming odds' may have become monotonous with repetition in this account of the actions of the battalion on that disastrous day, 5 June, but no other words can adequately describe these events.

And what of the 8/Argylls while all this was going on? We know that the men, led by Lieutenant Colonel Hamish Grant, were on the left of their sister battalion, the 7/Argylls, but by the morning of 6 June Grant was beginning to realize that his Battalion had been overrun. He knew that C and D Companies were still holding out but, as with Franleu, the bulk of

Lanchères Churchyard Cemetery: grave markers of some of the men of the 8/Argylls.

the Germans had by-passed them on their way south. He had not heard at all from A and B Companies since the previous day and as far as he was concerned the Battalion was now effectively Headquarters Company, three carriers and a collection of signallers, clerks and pioneers, numbering some 140 men.

At 4.00pm Major Lorne Campell arrived in Brutelles with orders for A Company to move back to Woignarue but was horrified to find the village already occupied by the Germans. Campbell, realizing he was cut off, ordered his men into Ault and found to his surprise a platoon of the 6/Royal Scots Fusiliers and about fifteen French marines ensconced around the lighthouse on the cliffs above the village. Campbell decided to move and attempt to get back to his Division; at last light, at the head of the column, he proceeded to march the whole way on a compass bearing of 146 degrees. He changed direction twice to avoid suspected trouble spots, hoping to reach the Bois de Bouvaincourt before daylight. Having failed to reach the wood and only the outskirts of Menelies, nightfall saw Campbell opting to make for a crossing on the River Bresle.

Major Lorne Campell.

Towards daylight the column was nearing the high ground overlooking the Bresle when they were challenged by German sentries; but the Argylls were soon over the high ground, not having taken any casualties in the process. Eric Linklater describes the moment they reached the safety of the British lines:

Le Lieu Dieu lay below them. A rearguard was left under Captain Webb, and B Company formed up for an attack. The village was reconnoitred and it became apparent that the Argylls had come into No Man's Land. The morning mist lay in the valley. They hurried on and crossed the channels of the Bresle by the wreckage of two blown bridges, then waded a third stream. A rear party covered each crossing.

Once across the river the only imminent danger lay in death by friendly fire. Second Lieutenant Mackinnion volunteered to go forward with his patrol and it was he that made contact with the 4/Black Watch.

Major Lorne Campbell had accomplished a remarkable feat. He had led 200 men on a march of 14 miles behind enemy lines, moving at night and relying in his compass. Only three men had been lost and they had probably fallen asleep and been left behind. It was generally accepted that only

Major Campbell could have accomplished the march. His remarkable feat must surely go down alongside that of the 5/Gloucesters at Ledringhem and the 2/Dorsets at Festubert in 1940. Campbell was awarded a Distinguished Service Order (DSO) for the feat, Captain Webb and Second Lieutenant Mackinnon were each awarded the Military Cross (MC).

The 1/Lothians Withdraw

On 4 June the Regiment was holding a four mile front on the high ground overlooking the Somme with two of their squadrons on the front line. Just after 4.15am the C Squadron posts were attacked and Major Jimmy Dallmayer, commanding A Squadron, immediately dispatched a troop of Carriers to assist them. He may have regretted this decision, as at 5.30am his own positions were attacked by the Germans. A Squadron was holding 2,000 yards of line with sixty-five men, made up of Squadron HQ at Tourbières and the carriers of Second Lieutenant Bobby Dundas. The two troops of light tanks and most of the carriers were in reserve some way back.

The German's attack originated from Mareuil and probably took an advanced post by surprise, as no gunfire was heard coming from it. But the surprise was on the German side when they rounded a corner and came face to face with a disabled French tank, Major Dallmayer's account recorded the next moments:

> They caught sight of the French tank. There were two men in front, the leading man put up his hands, the second man shot him in the back. We shot the second man. The Germans retreated and some made their way through the houses and back gardens up the ridge on the north side of the valley, others towards the Somme. Once established there they opened fire with mortars and machine guns.

Realizing the attack was now on his left flank, Dallmayer sent a dispatch rider to order Dundas to move at once to the left sector but Dundas's troop had been attacked, with only one carrier surviving. Dundas was immediately instructed to get in touch with Regimental Headquarters to request a counter-attack against the German push; Lieutenant Colonel Ansell sent his regrets and said that Dallmayer should hold on. Mike Ansell was fighting his own battle:

> Early on the morning of 4 June, Jimmy Dallmeyer came through (by wireless) to say he was being attacked in strength; almost immediately the same [message came] from Sandy Usher. At first light I decided to move out of our village and take up a position in the woods just behind. Within minutes of our withdrawal the village had been shelled and bombed. By 9.00am A Squadron was thick into the heavy fighting, Bobbie Dundas and Adam Thorburn-Brown had been killed, and it became obvious that the enemy could not be stopped from passing through . . . I told division we would be unlikely to be able to hold on –

only to be told in turn that we must not withdraw before six that evening. I remember thinking, 'Hell, how can we stay here?

Two tanks had been sent up by Ansell to help with the withdrawal and Dallmeyer asked Thorburn-Brown to cover the Mareuil road with one tank while Bobby Dundas went in the other to make contact with the remainder of the patrol who had been pinned down by the weight of fire. Dundas and Lieutenant Adam Thorburn-Brown paid for this excursion with their lives, while the rest of the squadron, using a track through the woods, escaped after a march of some 10 miles and rejoined the Regiment at Oisemont, to the right of the 2/Seaforths.

A Squadron's casualties were forty out of sixty-five men, including two officers killed and one captured; C Squadron lost one killed and two taken prisoner; while B Squadron lost Second Lieutenant Tighe and three men to shellfire. (27-year-old Second Lieutenant the Hon Robert St-John Dundas and 36year-old Adam Thorburn-Brown are commemorated on the Dunkirk Memorial; Second Lieutenant Brian Tighe is commemorated in the same cemetery.)

Despite the permission to withdraw, Weygand's original instruction was that there was to be no withdrawal from the Bresle; something would have to be done if the Allied troops were not to be cut off by the Germans.

The first determined attack of **6 June** was targeted against the 1/Lothians at Oisemont, where B and C Squadrons were in a position holding the

(*Left*) Lieutenant Colonel Mike Ansell. The photograph was taken in 1951, after he was blinded. (*Right*) Adam Thorburn-Brown.

railway line. At dawn that day General Fortune had rung Ansell to impress upon him the need to hold their position until darkness:

> Just before dawn I was woken with orders from General Fortune to hold the village until told to withdraw. The Lothians were to cover the right of the Highland Division and I was to make contact with the French. I went to get my bearings at first light, finding what was in fact a small town, completely deserted, with a railway running north and south; near the station stood three large gasometers. Absolutely flat arable land lay in the direction of the Germans for 800 yards, then a wood. Patrols moved out meeting nothing. We searched south 7 or 8 miles for the French, but never a sign; so obviously we were the right flank and all was open beyond us!

It was a beautiful sunny day and for a few hours the Lothians could forget about the war. B Squadron was dug in by the railway line but they had seen movement in the woods. Also with B Squadron was a section of the 7/Royal Northumberland Fusiliers, a machine gun regiment like the 1/Kensingtons, which was armed with the .303 Vickers machine gun. At 7.00pm Ansell received word from Division that it was imperative that the regiment hold on until midnight to give the infantry who were holding the line some 10 miles to the rear time to withdraw. Ansell again:

> Once again I remember thinking, 'Hell, what a hope. We'll be over-run.' I went up front to see Watty and Sandy. Oisemont was hardly a health resort: gasometers blazing, shell holes for a street and the church flattened with the rest of the buildings. Just as it was getting dark, shelling and strafing re-doubled and from out of the wood came the German infantry en masse – I might have said in a crowd: they could have been leaving a football match. For a time they made it easy for us; they could never get across that flat open country. We poured out fire with every weapon we'd got. Still they came on; still we stopped them. As night closed in we knew we'd held them up, and at midnight we withdrew.

For this defence of the open flank of the Division Lieutenant Colonel Ansell earned his nickname 'Glory'and was awarded the DSO. Casualties were light and, apart from three tanks lost, the only officer killed was Second Lieutenant Ian Lawrie of C Squadron. (He is buried in Oisemont Communal Cemetery, Grave 34.)

Sharing the line with the Lothians were the 2/Seaforths from 152 Brigade. They too had a peaceful morning. When the Germans launched their attack from the wood and began advancing on Oisemont Sergeant John Mackenzie recorded the suicidal nature of their advance:

> The German infantry tried to assault on our right, coming on in waves and dying in mass formation. For hours it was mass slaughter, every

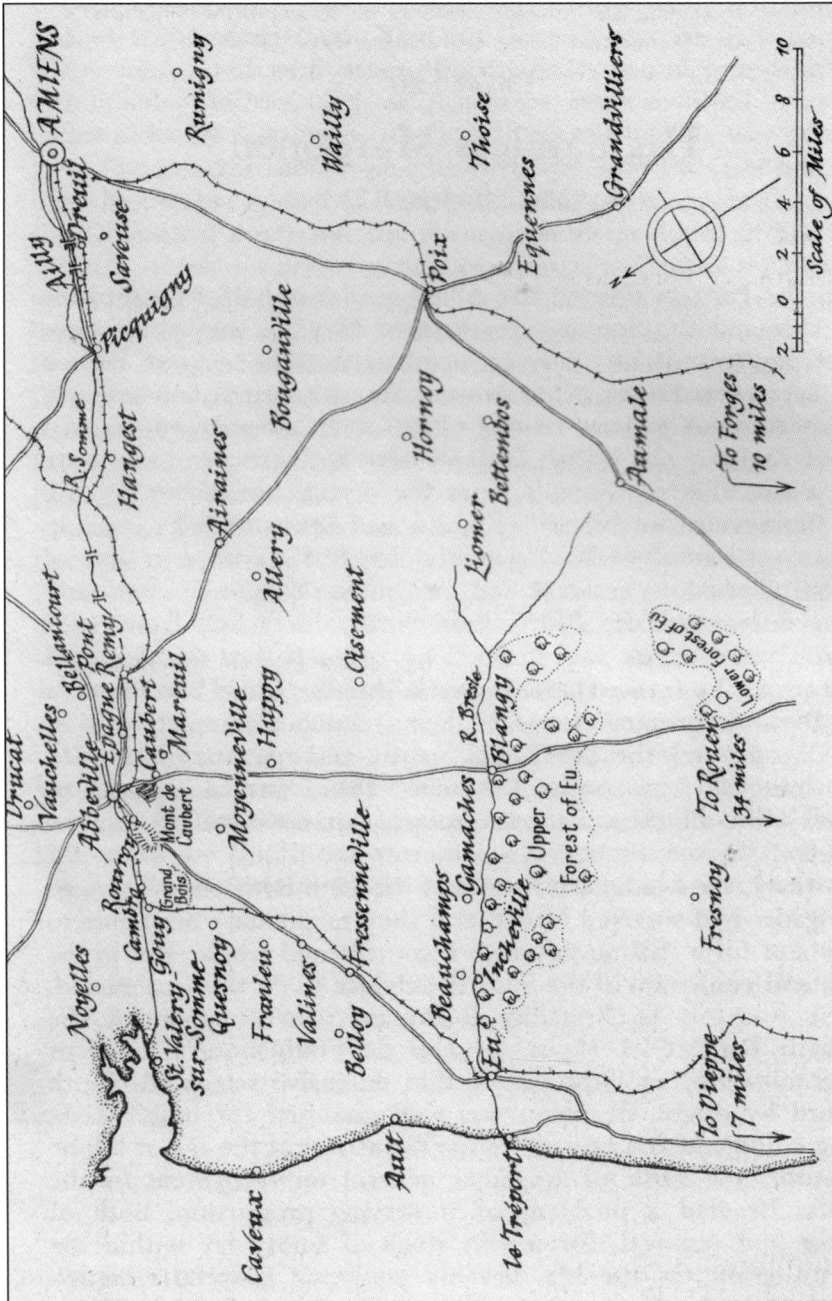

A **map from** *Destination Dunkirk* showing Oisemont and the area around the River Bresle.

Bren and machine gun taking its toll, Roddy Graham (the Mortar Officer) and his mortars plastered the wood as the enemy emerged from it. It was the one occasion on which we really caught Jerry starting off on the wrong foot – and we took full advantage. We had to put up with a lot from his planes, but B Company had all its riflemen firing at them and kept them at a good height.

All companies were able to break off successfully and the whole withdrawal was covered by Second Lieutenant Bill Cheyne's carriers.

The 4/Queens Own Cameron Highlanders

The 4/Camerons were on the railway line as well and Colour Sergeant Gregor MacDonald, although wounded in the head, was detailed to take the remaining men of B Company back to the Oisemont railway line from Battalion Headquarters at Huchenneville. Here they observed two captured 4/Seaforth trucks attempting to get up close to their positions:

Our line of approach was a narrow sandy road running at right angles to the railway line, crossing it at a level crossing and continuing across hayfields until is disappeared in a forest half a mile away. From the railway line we had an excellent field of fire and we started to dig-in without delay. For our defence we had twenty-four rifles, two sub-machine guns and two Bren guns. The Brigade anti-tank platoon had

The former level crossing on the Oisemont railway that could easily have been the one occupied by Colour Sergeant Gregor MacDonald.

sited a light Hotchkiss anti-tank gun on out left flank. About eleven o'clock in the forenoon two-hundred-weight trucks emerged from the woods on out front. Having the only field glasses I kept them in focus and was relieved to find they carried the 4/Seaforth identification plates. However, when they were about 200 yards from our position they suddenly pulled up and two German mortar sections alighted with their weapons and disappeared into the long grass. We immediately opened up with our Brens and one of the vehicles had trouble getting away. The other took cover in a depression and we observed the two sections piling into it before heading back to the shelter of the woods.

Brigadier Staney-Clarke, commanding 154 Brigade, had moved his Headquarters by 6.00 on 5 June to Dargnies, some 2 miles north east of the Bresle. This move was accompanied by the artillery, less two troops of 17/Field Regiment still at Ochancourt. Contact had been lost with 153 Brigade on the right, and some enemy forward units were reported to be between Dargnies and the Bresle. There was little hope of holding this line and the Division had orders to delay the German advance beyond it for a limited period only. There were simply not enough firepower or troops to meet the enemy's attack. Some of the bridges over the Bresle had already been blown whilst 152 Brigade had fallen back to the railway line running from Oisemont to the main road at Blagny, their numbers greatly diminished after the battle for the bridgehead at Abbeville.

At dawn on 6 June the Division was spread out on a line running 5 miles from the Bresle, which was in front of it. It became clear to the troops that General Fortune could hope for nothing better than a rearguard action, by which he hoped to punish and delay the enemy advance and keep in touch with the French, who were falling back on his right.

That day a divisional order was issued, confirming the withdrawal to the Bresle that evening with the intention of securing the line Senarpont and Le Treport, which was at the mouth of the Bresle, on the coast. Bridges were identified for use by different units and all bridges would be demolished by the Royal Engineers when the last unit had crossed. By the early hours of 7 June the Division was safely behind the River Bresle.

The crossing was not without incident, however. The 4/Black Watch, *en-route* for the Beauchamps crossing point, discovered a group of enemy had beaten them to it. Fortunately the Battalion's anti-tank platoon had also been sent there and managed to drive the Germans off. At Ponts-et-Marais, near Eu, the 6/Royal Scots facilitated the last minute detonation of the bridge by covering the demolition party and knocking out a light tank with an anti-tank rifle.

But their days were numbered on the Bresle; for with the German armour already in Rouen by 9 June and the bridges across the Seine blown, it was too late to make a stand on the Bresle.

The River Bresle at Eu.

Cemeteries Visited:

Abbeville Communal Cemetery Extension. The town fell to the Germans at the end of May 1940 and was retaken in 1944. This is a large cemetery containing men of the First World War as well as those from 1940. The headstones are carefully placed at the far end of the cemetery on the right of the access track and the 1940 graves are to the left of the Cross of Sacrifice. The cemetery also contains a number of French headstones.

Mareuil-Caubert Communal Cemetery. On Rue du Général Leclerc (D503) and situated on the side of a hill, this cemetery contains a great many unknown soldiers amongst its 157 Graves. Amongst those who have been identified, two brothers from Cromarty, William (1.C.3) and James Scott (2.C.19), aged 25 and 29, rest here, both killed on 6 June.

Franleu Churchyard Cemetery. The cemetery can be found on Rue des Pommiers. From the schoolhouse, on the opposite side of the road, head along the road/track and enter the churchyard to find the war graves on the left. There are twenty-six headstones, mainly of 7/Argyll and Sutherland Highlanders but also a few from the Royal Artillery and Gordon Highlanders. Those of you who are entering the churchyard from the front will find the war graves behind the church.

Mons-Boubert Communal Cemetery. The cemetery is on the western side of the village, on the by-road to Catigny. There is only one identified soldier of 1940 here, Private George Henderson, killed between 4 and 5 June; the other grave is of an unidentified soldier. The two graves are at the far end of the cemetery.

Oisemont Communal Cemetery. Located just off the D93, in the centre of town on Rue Latte á Huguenots and marked by the green gates. Oisemont was the start line for the attack of 27 May carried out by the 10/Hussars. The cemetery contains three Second World War graves and one from the First World War. Here lie: Gunner Robert Green of 204 Battery, 51 Anti-Tank Regiment; Fusilier John Hogarth of the 7/Royal Northumberland Fusiliers; and Second Lieutenant Ian Lawrie of the 1/Lothians. All three men died on 6 June 1940.

Mareuil-Caubert Communal Cemetery.

Oisemont Communal Cemetery. Second Lieutenant Ian Lawrie's grave is in the centre of the three headstones.

Ramburelles Churchyard Cemetery. There is only one British burial here, that of 29-year-old Captain John Wyndham Malet of the 10/Royal Hussars, who was killed on 27 May at Huppy. The grave can be located in the south eastern corner of the churchyard.

Grandcourt War Cemetery. A small cemetery, east of Dieppe on the road from Blagny-sur-Bresle to Fresnoy. It contains only fifty-four graves, four of whom remain unidentified.

Chapter 6

Beyond the Bresle

Rommel was in the process of carrying out another advance, and the 51st Division was, for all intents and purposes, shortly to be cut off. Fortune knew that the only way to save his Division was by evacuation from Le Havre and the plan was to reach the harbour by 13 June. Many historians believe that the greatest tragedy of the whole campaign was General Fortune's choice of Le Havre over Dieppe as the harbour for evacuation. With the panzer divisions in or close to Rouen it was all but inevitable that they would be in Le Havre by 13 June; Dieppe, on the other hand, was a day's journey away.

The question naturally arises: did Fortune make a fundamental error of judgment in choosing St Valery-en-Caux over Dieppe? Probably not is the blunt answer, as it was believed at the time that Dieppe was unsuitable for embarkation because of bomb damage and mines at the entrance to the harbour. However, on 9 June Dieppe still had a partially functioning harbour and a signal confirmed this, although it said that Le Havre was better for heavy supplies. Another reason why Dieppe was not considered is that block ships had apparently been sunk in the harbour. This was functionally untrue, for if boats could land supplies they were capable of using Dieppe to evacuate troops.

Whatever the case a question mark must remain over Fortune's choice of embarkation port. If Fortune and his staff were unaware of the capacity that Dieppe harbour still possessed, then it should have been made clear to them by the Admiralty and or the War Office. The fact that it was not

Dieppe in 1940.

Le Havre in 1940.

is perhaps explained by the British government's desire to keep the 51st Division in the war; but this is unlikely.

Fortune, above all else, was a career soldier and was instilled with a sense of staunch obedience to his superior officers. In this case his superiors were the French and they had not given him permission to use Dieppe; in fact they had given him orders to retire over the Seine, an order his own government had endorsed. If Fortune had been given the right of appeal, he might have felt, like Gort did further north, that he had a duty to save his men by embarking them at Dieppe. In the event he, with the complicity of Général Ihler, headed towards Le Havre. On 7 June Général Ihler was given command of the new IX Corps by Altmayer; included in his new command was the British 51st Division, the French 31st and 40th Divisions and the remnants of the 2nd and 5th DCLs.

Orders were given to withdraw from the Bresle to the next river, the River Béthune. From now on it was to be a race to get to Le Havre before German armour got to the Channel coast and blocked the Division's escape route. To conform to the new line on the Béthune, the Division occupied a line from Arques-la-Bataille to Dieppe. As far as Dieppe was concerned, the 2/7 Duke of Wellingtons were providing the garrison of Dieppe and shortly afterwards came under the command of 152 Brigade.

Général Maurice Ihler.

Rommel

The tanks of the 7th Panzer Division were only about 30 miles from Rouen when Rommel noted in his diary that they were near Sigy and the River Andelle. The tone of his diary illustrates his 'up front' attitude, a remarkable contrast to his French counterparts:

> While the 25th Panzer Regiment now took possession of the hills around Menerval, the 37th Reconnaissance Battalion was ordered to reconnoitre west and south west as far as the River Andelle, on either side of Sigi (Sigi-en-Bray) and to get its main force up to Mesangueville as its next objective. After satisfying myself that the Panzer Regiment had occupied the important hills around Menerval, I drove to Captain Schultz's panzer company, which had been ordered to head forward into the wooded country west of Saumont as far as the main track intersection. The appearance of German troops on the main road from Paris to Dieppe near Forges-les-Eaux had already sealed the fate of many French vehicles. By the time I arrived well over forty vehicles had been picked up and traffic was still arriving from both directions. Panzer Company Schultz had also had great success in the woods east of Saumont, where a large ammunition depot had been captured.

Rommel had fortunately chanced upon a spot for his advance that was between the remnants of the two armoured brigades. The Andelle was held thinly by the Beauman Division, a force of nine infantry battalions made up of Lines of Communication troops which had been hastily cobbled together along a sixty mile line from from Dieppe to the Seine. It had no artillery and few anti-tank guns; but the remnants of the 1st Armoured Division managed to scrape together ninety or so tanks to support the centre of the line. Rommel pierced the Andelle Line the next day at a point between the two brigades of the Armoured Division. The Beauman Division withdrew southwards and succeeded in slipping away across the Seine at Gallion.

At 5.30pm on 10 June German tanks were reported to be approaching Dieppe from Totes, which the French were believed to be holding. An hour or so later information confirmed that eight enemy tanks were within 6 miles of La Chaussée. Two pounder anti-tank guns were ordered to block the road and at 8.00pm the tanks were halted. News also came in that enemy tanks had been seen west of the River Durdent, whilst there was more bad news to come. At 11.00pm on 10 June a wireless lorry sent to maintain contact with Ark Force had run into reconnaissance troops of the 7th Panzer Division on the main road to Fécamp. The signaller just managed to get a message off that the enemy were now between the 51st Division and Le Havre before he was cut off. In order to establish the 7th Panzer Division's strength and dispositions, the 1/Lothians, accompanied by an anti-tank battery and a platoon of the Kensingtons, were sent forward:

> As definite news of the enemy was very vague, a mixed force was hastily gathered together at Divisional HQ consisting of the Lothian

Erwin Rommel.

and Border Horse, commanded by Lt. Col. Lord Ansell, an anti-tank battery of 51/Anti-Tank Regiment, commanded by Major Peacock, and a machine gun platoon of A Company of the Kensingtons, under the command of Lt. Wood. This force was to proceed along three parallel roads towards Fécamp and Le Havre in three bounds and to report each bound clear to Divisional HQ, and deal, if possible, with any opposition. The Division was to follow up gradually, ready for instant battle, with the French IX Corps on the flank. The recce unit threaded its way towards Fécamp and only on the left flank was serious opposition encountered and then it was suitably dealt with. Nearing Fécamp it became obvious that there were considerable (enemy) forces between this town and Le Havre and there was no alternative but to prepare to defend St Valery and trust in the navy.

The crossings of the Durdent at Cany and Veulettes were certainly found to be in enemy hands and the 1/Lothians suffered casualties here. Rommel had reached the Channel coast at Les Petits Dalles in the afternoon of 10 June. His orders were to strike north to the sea, with light reconnaissance vehicles and armoured cars pushing ahead of his main armour.

A slightly different account of the reconnaissance is offered by Lieutenant Reg Wood of the 1/Kensingtons:

Soon afterwards, however, firing was heard on out left and that squadron reported German tanks in the vicinity across their front and possibly spreading toward us. The column was stopped, and A/T (Anti-Tank) gunners rushed their guns out and we mounted our Vickers alongside them. Heavy firing continued for some time until the message came through that the opposition had been liquidated. Soon after we had moved on a message came through from the squadron on the coast road for a M/G (machine gun) section, as a number of enemy infantry were on a hill outside a village. This was sent off and when we heard the obstacle had been overcome we moved on again and later reached the outskirts of Fécamp ... Fécamp was blazing as its oil tanks had been bombed

Lieutenant Reg Wood in 1945.

a few hours previously but there were several British Merchant ships lying off the shore. Near the harbour we met some sailors who said they had orders to wait and see if anyone wanted to be evacuated. We explained the situation to them and asked for the town major; but that

Men of the 7/Argylls on the River Bresle.

individual was drunk and had barricaded himself in his office and was refusing to come out. A message now came through that the squadron on the Route Nationale had encountered heavy opposition and had seen large formations of enemy tanks approaching Fécamp. We therefore withdrew and harboured for the night in a small village near Veules-les-Roses.

The four bridges over the Durdent between Veulettes and Cany were now either destroyed or occupied by units of Rommel's 7th Panzer Division: the escape route to Le Havre was now definitely cut off. However, by 6.00pm General Fortune still had no definite news that the 1/Lothians had failed in their attempt to secure the Durdent. Consequently, he sent a signal to the War Office that said that enemy AFVs had intercepted his communications with Fécamp and he was still unclear about the situation. It was around this time that Major James Grant, the *de facto* commander of the 2/Seaforths, arrived at Divisional HQ at Ouville. He suggested to Fortune that instead of trying to hold the line of the Durdent it would make much better sense to hold the heights west of St Valéry-en-Caux. After some consideration Fortune agreed and issued orders to hold a line from Le Tot on the coast to the village of Neville. Circumstances had forced Fortune to choose St Valéry-en-Caux as the main point of embarkation.

Early the next morning a message came through that it was hoped to evacuate the Division and the French that night from St Valéry-en-Caux, as it was now impossible to get through to Le Havre.

Chapter 7

Ark Force

The narrative needs to return to 9 June, the day on which Ark Force was formed. Le Havre is a large town and port on the Channel coast and in 1940 was one of the main supply ports for the BEF taking in stores, ordnance and motor transport as well as troops. Indeed, it was returning to a situation which it had known only too well during the First World War, when it was a major logistics hub for the BEF from the outset of that war.

Le Havre is situated about 35 miles west of St Valery-en-Caux. It had a small British garrison, commanded by Lieutenant Colonel Butler. Once it became known that German armour was in Rouen, General Fortune realised that any chance of evacuation was now going to have to take place from Le Havre. Lieutenant Colonel Butler would need reinforcements if the town was to be defended. It was a memorable evening, a flight of German bombers drumming though the clear sky towards Le Havre and the warm summer sun bearing down on the officers of the divisional command. This was also the day when Weygand made his cryptic comment: *Nous sommes au dernier quart d'heure. Tenez bon.*

The Conference at Arques-la-Bataille

On the same day the commanders of the units of the Division gathered at a Divisional Conference at Arques-la-Bataille; General Fortune outlined the events of the morning. He told them that their only escape route was via Le Havre but, because there was every likelihood of the Germans arriving at Le Havre before 13 June, he was sending out a strong force – Ark Force – under the command of Brigadier Arthur Stanley-Clarke.

His job was to join up with the French and secure the route to Le Havre. It was a slim hope that Ark Force would then allow the Division to pass through it on their way to embarkation and would reconnoitre an inner line of defence around the port. The inner line would be protected by a rearguard. Although consisting of almost half of the Division, Ark Force contained units that were much weaker than the remainder; whilst all the regular battalions, the armoured regiment and most of the anti-tank guns were to remain with the Division; the name given to Stanley-Clarke's command was Ark Force. Lieutenant Colonel Ansell was present at the divisional conference:

> In a small schoolroom Victor Fortune explained we would now retire to Le Havre. One brigade under Stanley-Clark was to fall back to cover us. We knew well we didn't have a hope of getting to Le Havre.

An aerial photograph of Arques-la-Bataille today.

Fortune's orders to Stanley-Clarke were terse and to the point:

> Should it be apparent that enemy attack from the south or east has made any organized evacuation from Havre impossible, you will withdraw and evacuate at Havre as many of your force as you can, destroying all abandoned material whilst taking off as much material as can be carried.

Stanley-Clarke was then ordered to leave the conference and form Ark Force immediately. It was to prepare to defend Le Havre, as from here it was hoped to evacuate the Division. No sooner had the Divisional Conference concluded than the advanced elements of Ark Force were on their way to Fécamp. Ark Force took its name from Arques-la-Bataille, a partly anglicized version of the town where the conference was held and with a nodding reference to Noah's Ark. The HQ of 154 Brigade, the town was set just south of Dieppe.

The Units of Ark Force

Nearly half of the Division was chosen to head south to Le Havre and, equipped with his orders from General Fortune, Stanley-Clarke left the beleaguered Division with the following units:

A Brigade from the Beauman Division
4/Border Regiment
5/ Sherwood Foresters
4/East Kent Regiment (Buffs)

154 Brigade

4/The Black Watch
7/The Argyll and Sutherland Highlanders
8/The Argyll and Sutherland Highlanders
6/Royal Scots Fusiliers (Pioneers)

Royal Artillery

17th Field Regiment RA
75th Field Regiment RA
204/Anti-tank Battery from the 51/Anti-tank Regiment
1/Kensingtons (Machine gunners, less two companies)

Royal Engineers

236/Field Company
237/Field Company
239/Field Park Company
213/Field Company

Field Ambulance

154/Field Ambulance
Detachments from 525, 526 and 527 RASC Companies

By sending Ark Force ahead to Le Havre, Fortune had in fact committed what is militarily considered the cardinal error of splitting his force. One might presume that he had seen an opportunity to combine a tactical reconnaissance with the chance of giving a large percentage of his men the opportunity of escaping via Le Havre. There again, Lieutenant Colonel Butler's plea for reinforcements should not be discounted, which may have prompted Fortune's decision. Whatever the reasons, at a stroke Fortune had saved nearly half of his Division from destruction. He must have known that the part of the Division that was remaining behind was doomed to death or capture. His conclusion was that, given the tactical position he now found himself in, together with the speed that IX Corps was likely to make on foot, he would be unable to make Le Havre in time to be evacuated. In his signal to the War Office at 11.37pm on 9 June he outlined those fears:

> Sending rearguard to reinforce French on line Fécamp-Lillebonne. My speed depends on French movement, about 20km a day. Tomorrow morning line should be Dieppe ... If enemy break through French or cuts me off from Le Havre, will attempt pivot on one of the northern ports.

Slow progress to Fécamp

Due to the exceptionally high volume of traffic on the road to Fécamp, including the very large number of refugees pushing their carts and prams, the slower elements of Ark Force did not reach the town until late. The force was travelling for a time in broad daylight and it was only luck that prevented the convoy from being attacked by the Luftwaffe. In fact

German bombers head for Le Havre.

The slower elements did not reach Fécamp until much later in the day.

A huge cloud of smoke had spread for miles and provided cover for Ark Force.

German bombing had set the oil containers in the town ablaze and a huge cloud of smoke spread for miles, happily enough providing cover for Ark Force. Nevertheless, two Companies from A Brigade failed to make it to Fécamp, one from the 4/Buffs and the other from 1/5 Foresters. They were held up by traffic and lost their battalions in the confusion. They then returned and came under the command of 152 Brigade.

Eric Linklater later wrote that the night of 9/10 June was exceptionally difficult:

> At night the transport drivers on the coast road to Fécamp had to navigate a darkness so thick and evil smelling as almost to be palpable. The roads, as they were at all times, were clotted with refugees, and French batteries were also on the move. Ark Force fumbled its way between gross but invisible obstacles and struggled through black confusion to its goal.

There was heavy enemy bombing during the night; although several bombs were dropped on the Force, no damage was done. Ark Force Operation Order No. 2 was issued on 11 June; it began by stating that enemy forces had reached Fécamp on 10 June but there had been no enemy movement from Lillebonne to Bolbec. French troops were holding the railway line from Lillebonne to Fécamp and the decision was made to create two further defensive lines.

93

These lines, running north-west to south-east, were situated roughly north-east of Le Havre and were to be held to the last man. The forward line was roughly 10 miles from Le Havre and was garrisoned by A Brigade of the Beauman Division, 17/Field Regiment, one troop of 75/Field Regiment and one company of the 1/Kensingtons. In command was Brigadier Malcolm Green, who had a temporary Headquarters at St Aubain. The second line was much closer to Le Havre. It formed a defensive pocket around the port and was commanded by Lieutenant Colonel Grant, who had his headquarters in the Forêt de Montgeon. It was held by the remnants of 154 Brigade, 75/Field Regiment – less one troop, 204/Anti-Tank Battery, one company of the 1/Kensingtons and two companies from the Le Havre garrison. The men were left in little doubt as to what was expected of them: *positions will be held until definite orders have been received. Under no circumstances will sub units withdraw until such orders have been received.*

154/Field Ambulance was positioned in the Forêt de Montgeon, with access to 11/General Hospital in the Palais des Règates. The Forêt de Montgeon also housed the main supply dump, from which troops could draw rations and petrol. Unfortunately, there were no stocks of ammunition available as most of the ordnance had already been cleared. Brigadier Stanley-Clarke gave out new orders in the hope that General Fortune might still be able to make it to Le Havre:

He knew then that the remaining brigades of the 51st were in a desperate plight. He knew that Fortune meant to keep step with the French 31st Division, which could only march at a speed of 18km per day, and he knew that before they could arrive he would have to fight to keep the port open. But he was still hopeful that Fortune and his tattered battalions would get through.'

On the night of 10 June there were repeated air attacks on Le Havre and which continued through 11 June. The troops were, however, encouraged by the sight of three Fairey Battles, light bombers, which flew low over the town. There was still no news of the enemy land forces until late afternoon, when Ark Force stood to arms on receiving a report that German tanks were advancing on Fécamp. Fortunately no tanks appeared

Brigadier Stanley-Clarke Gives the Order for Evacuation
After all hope that the remainder of the Division might make it to Le Havre were quashed by the movement of Rommel's tanks, Stanley-Clarke reluctantly gave the order to prepare for evacuation:

Then the Navy reported that the other Brigades were completely cut off, and an attempt would be made to embark them at St Valery. Thereupon arrangements were immediately made for the evacuation of Ark Force and the garrison of Le Havre.

Rommel and his tanks of the 7th Panzer Division were not far behind.

All transport was destroyed at the dockside by driving the trucks into each other; the car belonging to the Commanding Officer of the 6/Royal Scots Fusiliers was preserved until last: Fusilier Hay, its driver, reportedly asked another Fusilier to destroy the vehicle.

Ark Force had missed being cut off with the rest of the division by a matter of hours; it had been a close run thing and we can only imagine the situation at Ark Force Headquarters, situated at Rue Felix Fauré, as the code-word to begin the evacuation was transmitted. (The code-word for the evacuation to begin was 'Whoopee', evidently devised by a person with a sense of humour!)

Fighting took place in the forward line near Fècamp before troops manning the line were ordered to withdraw, which they did successfully, protected somewhat by the low cloud and rain. The inner defensive line was to have withdrawn at midday on 12 June but, at the request of the French, this was delayed by a further twelve hours to allow various French units to reach Le Havre. Eventually this line withdrew, regardless of the intense air activity from German aircraft. Ark Force was successfully evacuated from Le Havre from the evening of 12 June, the 1/Kensingtons were embarked on the SS *Lady of Man* and found themselves at Southampton the next morning. Others were evacuated first to Cherbourg, where they joined Operation Cycle to transport then back to England. On

Brigade A of the Beauman Division were evacuated from Le Havre.

the nights of 11/12 and 12/13 June over 4,000 men of Ark Force were evacuated from Le Havre.

Operation Cycle

As the trap facing the 51st Division became ever more apparent, the British government was making attempts to salvage its troops. There were more than 160,000 British soldiers still in France. On 8 June the Admiralty was

The port of Le Havre was almost destroyed.

Elements of Ark Force pleased to be going home at last.

instructed to prepare for their evacuation. Still at large in the Le Havre peninsula were at least 1,200 men of the garrison at Le Havre and a number of Lines of Communication Troops guarding the supply dumps. Admiral Sir William James, Commander-in-Chief, Portsmouth was given the job of masterminding the planning and, as we know, Ark Force and associated troops were successfully evacuated from Le Havre.

Operation Cycle was not planned to include the 51st Division, for as far as the War Office knew the Highlanders were under the command of the French and the French had ordered IX Corps and the 51st Division to retreat to the Seine. But they did send two naval officers to join the 51st Division with a means of communication to keep in touch with HMS *Wanderer*, a destroyer off the French coast. These naval officers, Commander Elkins and Lieutenant Commander Elder, would 'keep an eye on the Division' and would also be on hand if arrangements were needed to proceed with evacuation. Elkins was later taken prisoner but managed to escape with Leslie Hulls.

Chapter 8

The Last Stand

Once the 51st Division had decided on St Valery-en-Caux as its evacuation point, Lieutenant Colonel Ansell of the 1/Lothians was ordered to make a reconnaissance of suitable positions for forming a perimeter around the town. Accordingly, he took the anti-tank commander and Lieutenant Reg Wood of the 1/Kensingtons in a Bren-gun carrier; they made a circle about 10 miles from the town and marked positions for the brigades of supporting troops.

Valery-en-Caux was, to say the least, inappropriate as an evacuation point. Situated at a break in the 300 foot high chalk cliffs, which run along much of this coast, the main road and railway line ran down to the town through a breach in the cliffs. It was a typical bottleneck, whose flanking beaches were only accessible through the town itself and then only at low tide. Any enemy seizing the cliff tops would dominate the town and harbour as well as the approaches from the sea. The harbour itself was small and dried out at low tide, whilst access to it from the sea was guarded by a narrow entrance between two lighthouses. St Valery-en-Caux was altogether a dangerous place to evacuate half of a division, let alone a whole one!

Operation Aerial

On 10 June the Navy sent three destroyers, *Bulldog*, *Boadicea* and *Ambuscade*, to investigate the potential of embarkation points from Fécamp to Dieppe. Near St Valery-en-Caux HMS *Ambuscade* was hit by an artillery battery from the 7th Panzer Division and at Veulettes, HMS *Boadicea* was heavily engaged by another battery while taking troops off the beaches.

That night boats were sent into the harbour and found no troops to be evacuated except a number of wounded, who were taken off by the tug

HMS *Boadicea*.

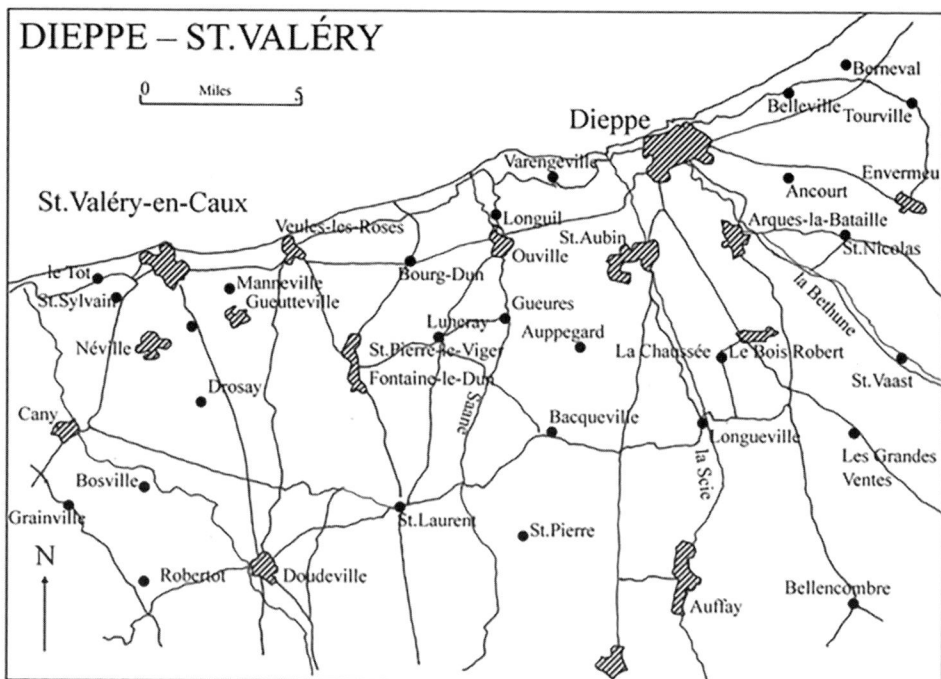

DIEPPE – ST.VALÉRY

0   Miles   5

Borneval
Belleville Tourville
Dieppe
Varengeville
Envermeu
Ancourt
St.Valéry-en-Caux
Veules-les-Roses
Longuil
Arques-la-Bataille
St.Nicolas
St.Aubin
le Tot
Ouville
Bourg-Dun
St.Sylvain
Manneville
Gueures
Gueutteville
Luneray
Néville
Auppegard
St.Pierre-le-Viger
La Chaussée Le Bois Robert
Drosay
Fontaine-le-Dun
St.Vaast
Cany
Bacqueville
Longueville
Bosville
Les Grandes
Ventes
Grainville
St.Laurent
St.Pierre
N
Robertot Doudeville
Bellencombre
Auffay

A map showing the country from Dieppe to St Valery-en-Caux.

Stalwart. On 11 June the destroyer HMCS *Restigouche* anchored offshore at Veules-les-Roses and took troops off the beaches, after which date any further daylight evacuations were forbidden.

The War Office still maintained that the 51st Division was under the command of IX Corps and therefore no evacuation could take place until the French agreed. However, it was tacitly acknowledged that by 11 June French arrangements had virtually collapsed and authority to evacuate was given. It is fortunate that Admiral James had not waited for the French to reply to Fortune's demands and had already assembled a fleet of over 300 ships and boats ready to evacuate the Division and what was left of the French IX Corps during the night of 11/12 June.

Fortune's signal to Admiral James on 11 June starkly evealed the difficulties he faced:

Intend to embark whole force tonight, Tuesday, provided sufficient ships and boat transport are available. If embarkation cannot be completed tonight, propose continuing am tomorrow, Wednesday. Consider air superiority is essential to neutralize shore batteries. Jumping ladders and nets required to assist embarkation. Time of commencement and beaches to use will be signalled. Embarkation tonight considered essential owing to probability of attack and shortage of rations, petrol and ammunition.'

100

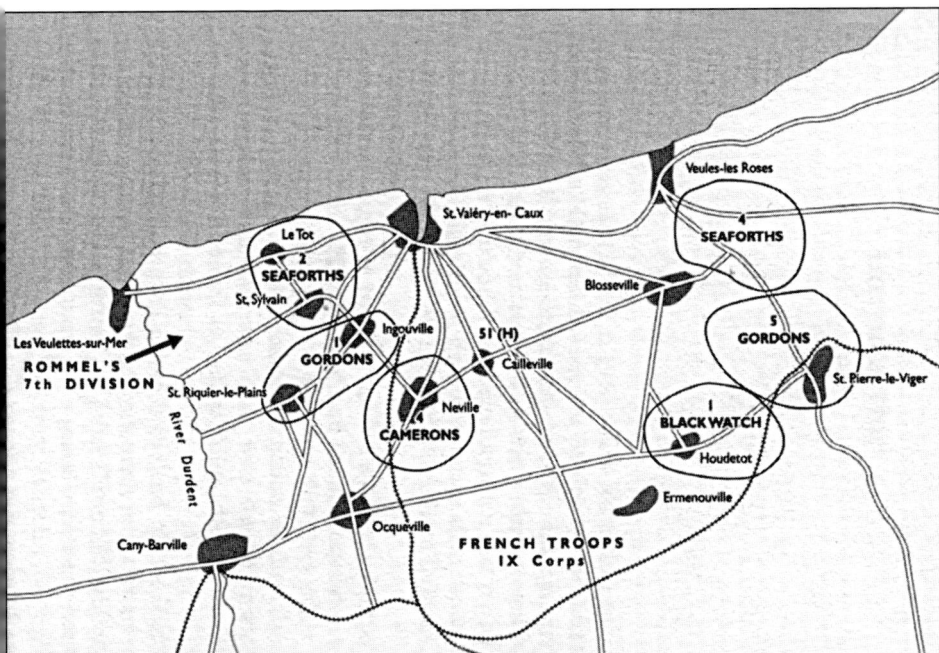

A map showing the final positions round St Valery-en-Caux. (After Second Lieutenant Ran Ogilvie, 1/Gordons.)

In the meantime, the remaining infantry battalions and artillery were to be deployed around St Valery in a semicircle, starting at Le Tot in the west and finishing at Veules-les-Roses in the east. On the western perimeter were the 2/Seaforths at Le Tot and St Sylvain, the 7/Norfolks and 1/Gordons at Ingouville and St Riquier-les-Plains and the 4/Camerons at Neville. Supporting these troops were 6 Platoon of the 1/Kensingtons. The eastern perimeter ran roughly north-south and started from Veules-les-Roses, where a French artillery regiment and the 2/7 Duke of Wellingtons were positioned. The 4/Seaforths were at Yelon, the 5/Gordons occupied St Pierre-le- Vigier. while half of the1/Black Watch were at Houdetot. All of the 1/Kensingtons of D Company were placed in support of the eastern perimeter. The southern perimeter was comprised of a mixture of French units and were supported by the remaining light tanks and carriers of the 1/Lothians.

Numerous accounts speak of the chaos that could be seen on the approach roads to St Valery. French transport ignored any attempt to enforce traffic control, the coast road was jammed solid for most of the night of 10/11 June and no attempt was made to adhere to the instructions of the British traffic control staff. Adding further confusion to the situation was the activity of the Luftwaffe in the skies above. Many units were delayed in reaching their positions especially along the eastern perimeter. Divisional HQ was at Cailleville; but this was considered too vulnerable

101

and it was later reopened in St Valery. At 1.00am on 11 June General Fortune issued the following message to his Division:

> The Navy will probably make an effort to take us off by boat, perhaps tonight, perhaps in two nights. I wish all ranks to realize this can only be achieved by the full co-operation of everyone, men may have to walk 5 or 6 miles. The utmost discipline must prevail. Men will board the boats with equipment and carrying arms. Vehicles will be rendered useless without giving away when this is being done. Carriers should be retained as the final rearguard. Routes back to the nearest highway should be reconnoitred and officers detailed as guides. Finally, if the enemy should attack before the whole force is evacuated, all ranks must realize that it is up to them to defeat them. He may attack with tanks, and we have quite a number of anti-tank guns behind. If the infantry can stop the enemy's infantry, then that is all that is required.

It was a tall order. Facing the Allied force around St Valery was five German divisions and a motorized brigade. These were: the 2nd Motorized Division, the 31st and 57th Infantry Divisions, the 11 Motorized Brigade and the 5th and 7th Panzer Divisions.

Owing to four battalions, having come straight from their positions on the Béthune River, ending up on the eastern perimeter, General Fortune was obliged to rationalize his outer defensive perimeter. 152 Brigade was ordered to take over the western perimeter, with its HQ at Caileville, while 153 Brigade was moved to the eastern line with its HQ at Blosseville. One battery of the 1/Royal Horse Artillery was also sent to the western

Funeral of a soldier in the 7th Battalion Royal Norfolks, who died in Stalag 21 in Poland 1941–2.

perimeter. Fortune also decided to move Divisional HQ into St Valery. Its location was moved firstly to a building near the railway station and then to a large house on the west side of the harbour. At the same time the Commanding Officer of the 7/Norfolks, Lieutenant Colonel Charles Debenham, was instructed to reconnoitre an inner defensive line in St Valery, with both flanks on the cliffs.

The Attack On the Perimeter

On 11 June the 7th Panzer Division, equipped with some 200 tanks and reinforced by the motorized infantry of the 6/Rifle Regiment, began their assault on the western perimeter, directly in line with the positions held by the 2/Seaforths at Le Tot and St Sylvain. It was well nigh impossible for the defenders to hold their own against tanks, armed only with Boyes Rifles. (The Boyes Rifle was an anti-tank weapon which was virtually ineffective against German armour.) Some artillery support was available and accounted for a few of the tanks but the remainder broke through and moved forward to the western cliffs, overlooking the town and harbour of St Valery. In a remarkably short space of time German infantry were probing the south-western approaches to the town.

Major James Murray Grant, the nominal commander of the 2/Seaforths, aware that the 2,500 yards of open ground that he had to defend would be impossible, had decided to concentrate his battalion among the two strong-holds of Le Tot and St Sylvain; both villages provided some sort of cover for his men. At St Sylvain Battalion HQ was based in a small orchard at the rear of the village; it was enclosed on three sides by a small earth bank, with woodland on the fourth side. The RAP was established just inside the enclosure in a lime-washed barn.

Having presented himself to General Fortune asking for artillery support, he was delighted to see an artillery observation officer and anti-tank officer installed at Le Tot. At 2.30pm a runner from A Company arrived at Battalion HQ with the news that over forty tanks were advancing on

A group of 2/Seaforths in 1939. Many of the soldiers in this photograph were killed or became prisoners.

Le Tot. At the same moment a message arrived from C Company that it had up to fifty tanks advancing on its front. The Mortar Platoon was rushed out and opened fire but within a few minutes the tanks had surrounded Battalion HQ and were firing at it on three sides. The Battalion suffered about thirty-five dead and wounded against damaging three of the enemy tanks, knocked out before the main attack swept on towards St Valery, whilst leaving a number of them to continue the battle at St Sylvain. Meanwhile, the Battalion's adjutant, Second Lieutenant Phillip Mitford, had gone to the RAP to receive medical attention when he was hit by a round from an enemy mortar:

> I was hit twice, by shrapnel in the foot and head, and I thought I had better get something done. But there were so many people in the Aid Post that I decided to leave the doctor, Mckillop, to carry on with the others. Seconds later the barn received a direct hit from a heavy mortar. Quite a few were killed inside and Mckillop was severely wounded – one leg was blown off and the other broken in three places. In spite of this he tried to direct operations and refused to be moved until the last man alive had been rescued.

The Medical Officer, Lieutenant Murdock Mckillop, and most of his staff had been either killed or wounded, Mckillop himself died later that evening. Major Grant noted in his diary that the flames and enemy fire

(*Left*) Lieutenant Phillip Mitford, taken after the war. (*Right*) Lieutenant Murdock Mckillop.

were causing even more casualties and it was impossible to get them out. Another soldier in the orchard was Second Lieutenant Colin Mackenzie, now the Battalion Intelligence Officer. His truck had been hit by machine-gun fire; he was in the process of re-joining the perimeter held by C Company when he was hit again:

> A bullet passed through the top of my tin hat and knocked me unconscious, although it didn't pass through my head, I didn't remember anything after that until I was woken by the screams of a very badly wounded soldier. By this time all the other troops that had been in this position had disappeared, and I, presumably, had been left for dead. Somehow I got this soldier into the ammunition truck and drove it to Battalion HQ, where the RAP was only a couple of yards away.

Major Grant was impressed with Mackenzie's gallantry but even more so when it was discovered that water and a case of biscuits were on the ammunition truck, which, according to Grant's diary, enabled the battalion to fight on for longer.

Many of the remaining troops at Le Tot were killed or wounded and a number were lost trying to work their way down the cliffs on 12 June. At St Sylvain the battle had died down by evening, but a considerable number of German tanks were still surrounding the village. Battalion HQ had moved twice. Major Grant brought the remaining men into a small perimeter and prepared to surrender.

On 12 June the 2/Seaforths were still in place at St Sylvain; no surrender had been offered and an occasional burst of fire from what the Seaforths presumed were German soldiers were the only signs that the enemy was still surrounding them. Then Company Quartermaster Sergeant Fields, who had been captured earlier, was sent into St Sylvain on a tank to deliver a demand that the besieged Seaforths surrender at once or be blown to pieces. Grant immediately called a conference in the cottage that was serving as an HQ. Phillip Mitford, the Battalion's adjutant, later wrote what happened:

> The alternatives were: (1) Fight it out in our present position. (2) Attempt a mass break-out in daylight. (3) Try to hold our position until nightfall and then attempt to escape in small parties, leaving the wounded to surrender. (4) Surrender. It was decided to carry on the fight from our present position.

However, Grant's mind was eventually changed and volunteers were called for to break-out in small parties, while the remainder of the battalion would surrender. One of the men who decided to break-out was Phillip Mitford:

> I was badly wounded in the arm and leg and I could hardly walk, but the arm didn't worry me and I was bloody well going to go. We set off

for the sea which we could see. It was a most gorgeous evening – the last thing we wanted – and we were in a cornfield. The next thing we saw was a German tank disgorging a whole lot of people. I think they must have heard us rustling through the corn because they came straight towards us. When they were about 10 yards away we decided it was all up and surrendered.

Second Lieutenant Colin Mackenzie was another who opted to break-out and this time the party got to the beach but then collapsed in a heap on the beach to sleep. They were captured by enemy troops scouring the beach.

The 1/Gordons were in an orchard at Ingouville that lay directly in the path of the panzer attack. Second Lieutenant Jimmy Dunlop was the first into action as commander of three anti-tank guns:

When the tanks advanced in sight of Battalion Headquarters they were almost at maximum range. I was with one gun that we had behind a haystack. When I went back to where the other guns were I found they had been knocked out by direct hits from the tanks. Also, a mortar bomb had landed while some silly clot was filling up a truck with petrol, causing a fire that spread to the ammunition truck for the anti-tank guns. Luckily we managed to get a couple of boxes of it which I took to the surviving gun.

During the remaining hours of daylight the Germans penetrated the ground between Battalion Headquarters and the forward companies. The wounded were moved across to a local chateau. Harry Wright, the Commanding Officer, was now cut off from his forward companies and he had received no orders for the evacuation which, as far as he knew, was to take place that night. Finally orders were brought by the Brigade Major of 152 Brigade but Wright had still not got word through to St Riquier. The man chosen to undertake this rather daunting task was Second Lieutenant Jimmy Dunlop. Before he had gone 500 yards he was hit in the leg by a German sniper, leaving Wright with no choice but to leave. About fifty badly wounded men were left behind in the chateau, looked after by the Medical Officer, Captain Nigel Altham, and some of the stretcher bearers, who volunteered to stay behind.

The three forward companies of the 1/Gordons were in a horseshoe shaped position on the edge of St Riquier. The flank of the panzer attack passed to their right but advanced straight over the top of D Company of the 7/Norfolks, who were dug in along a cornfield. An officer was sent out to assess the situation after the tanks had moved away and found almost total chaos. Heavy machine guns had split heads open and bodies were torn and dismembered. It must have been a horrific attack that, hopefully, the 7/Norfolks knew little about.

Wright was captured with the personnel of HQ and C Companies, as was Captain John Stansfield, the commander of D Company. Ogilvie

**Captain John Stansfield
commanded D Company.**

and 7 Platoon very nearly got away until the truck they had unexpectedly found was faced with two German tanks blocking the road. After a short skirmish, in which the truck crashed, they had no choice but to surrender. The German armoured attack of 11 June meant that any attempt to embark troops from St Valery was almost out of the question. The positioning of tanks and machine guns on the cliffs to the west of the town meant that the Germans commanded both the beaches and the harbour. Fortune had earlier persuaded Général Ihler to send a French regiment to guard the cliffs but by the time the advanced elements had reached them they withdrew in the face of the panzers. The inner perimeter, reconnoitred by Lieutenant Colonel Debenham of the 7/Norfolks, did not even have time to finish the task as fifteen tanks appeared on the top of the western cliffs. The speed of the German panzer attack was phenomenal.

Later the line was thickened by the addition of four companies of 7/Norfolks, together with two platoons of 1/Kensingtons and a platoon of 7/Royal Northumberland Fusiliers. However, this did not stop some German infantry working their way down the gardens and reaching the edge of the town. On the eastern perimeter the attack came at 4.00pm on 11 June, when units were bombed and machine gunned by the Luftwaffe; and then came the artillery barrage and armoured assault. Tanks came from the south-east and seemed hell bent on overcoming the 2/7 Duke of Wellingtons. Engaged by the 25-pounders of 23/Field Regiment, some tanks were destroyed but most got through, breaking the perimeter line and heading towards St Valery. The 2/7 Duke of Wellingtons was the first unit on the eastern perimeter to abandon its positions, probably because it assumed the road to St Valery had been cut and there was little time to waste before the evacuation got underway. Lieutenant Colonel Ernest Taylor, the Battalion's CO, ordered a withdrawal to the beach at Veules-les-Roses but did not, or forgot, to inform the 4/Seaforths of his intention. Taylor was captured with his Second-in-Command, Major Gerrard, when they became separated from the main body. The first thing Major Shaw-Mackenzie knew of their withdrawal was when a dispatch rider brought word to Battalion HQ:

He was in a state of breakdown and said, 'All the 2/7 Duke of Wellingtons have been killed'. I told him to calm himself and then questioned him. He said that he had been sent from his Battalion HQ on a message to one of the companies but had failed to find them. He had been along the whole line and found some men of the unit dead. He also said that he had failed to find Battalion HQ where he had left them.

The next thing that Shaw-Mackenzie knew was the arrival of his liaison officer from Brigade HQ, who handed him a note that read: *Thin out 2130 hrs, abandon positions 2200 hrs. Rdv at railway station St Valery for embarkation 0200 hrs.* By 3.00am the Battalion was underway and marched out of Yelon, arriving at St Valery-en-Caux intact.

The 1/Lothians
The southern perimeter was the weakest held, yet it remained relatively untouched on 11 June. Lieutenant Colonel Ansell was told that the 1/Lothians would act as rearguard until ordered to withdraw. Suspecting the rearguard would be unable to get away, Ansell asked Fortune for permission to break his Regiment into small groups to give his men the best chance of escaping. Fortune agreed. Ansell immediately set off to find the French cavalry regiment that was supposed to be holding the line nearby. He found the French commander in a long, low room overlooking an orchard:

> I became very angry as he waved away my questions, saying he did not know where his troops were and now it did not matter (as) he wished to surrender.'

A Vickers Mark VI Light Tank of the sort used by the 1/Lothians.

Ansell arrived back in time to find his unit packing up for withdrawal; as with all the units hoping for evacuation that night, they were ordered to destroy all their equipment. A particularly tragic episode involved some of the officers of the 1/Lothians who were attempting to escape. Lieutenant Colonel Ansell was heading south with Major Harry Younger, Captain Lord Hopetoun, the future Marquis of Linthigow, Second Lieutenant Kenneth Spreckley and RSM Waymark:

> We set off in the pouring rain, keeping close to the hedges and trees and looked for somewhere to lay up and rest until evening. We then made our mistake. We came across a farmhouse and climbed into the loft. Had it been fine we would have stayed in the open, under a hedge. There was plenty of straw (in the loft); gratefully we took off most of our sodden clothes and slept. A hail of bullets came through the floor and simultaneously the door of the loft flew open and I took the full blast of a Tommy-gun less than 10 feet away. We shouted and almost at once it stopped, then we heard voices in French and English below.

What had happened was that the French farmer had seen some men that he suspected to be Germans enter the left. A fugitive party of 1/Gordons had arrived at the farm and without any warning the Gordons opened fire on the loft. Hopetoun was down the ladder in a flash screaming at the assailants that they had shot their own side. The Gordon's sergeant beat a hasty retreat with his men, but the damage had been done. Younger was dead, Spreckley was wounded in the knee and Ansell was blinded. Convinced he was going to die, Ansell convinced his comrades to leave him and tell his wife, should any of them reach safety, that he loved her. Hopetoun and Spreckley were soon taken prisoner, Waymark chose to stay with Ansell, but both were taken prisoner. Ansell later had four fingers on his left hand amputated and was repatriated in 1943.

Younger is buried in the Franco-British Cemetery at St Valery-en-Caux.

The 1/Black Watch

The 1/Black Watch, who were at St Pierre-le-Viger, were also in action. The fragmentation of the Battalion was the result of a brigade order to reconnoitre a new line between Gueutteville-les-Grès and Cailleville. In preparation for this move, Lieutenant Colonel Eric Honeyman had moved three companies back to an orchard near Houdetot. At 7.00pm firing began in the rear and left flank and the Germans began working their way round the right flank. It was a tricky situation and Captain Berenger 'Bill' Bradford, the Battalion's adjutant, in the absence of Lieutenant Colonel Honeyman, told the French troops with whom he was sharing the position that he was considering a withdrawal. The French asked him to wait until dark and then withdraw. Bradford agreed. Taking more and more casualties from machine-gun and mortar fire, the Black Watch had to wait until darkness had fallen in order to withdraw with the French before making for

Gueutteville. As one platoon withdrew confusion reigned. Bradford recorded the last minutes of the withdrawal:

Captain 'Bill' Bradford, photographed in 1944.

Just before 2145 hrs, one platoon of A Company with its commander withdrew and caused confusion in the remainder of the company. Everyone got the idea that the enemy were right on top of us, and it was difficult to keep the men at Battalion HQ in their positions. B Company, I learned later, did not withdraw for some time, as its commander was trying to make arrangements for the wounded. As we had no stretcher and only one 8-cwt truck without a driver, this was impossible. Wounded were put on carriers, but I'm afraid many were left. It was awful.

After a march of 5 miles, during which they came under fire from German troops and then from French troops, who were withdrawing in the opposite direction, they reached Gueutteville and finally St Valery-en-Caux, which they could see ahead of them, marked by two great pillars of red smoke rising into the sky.

At Houdetot, the remainder of the 1/Black Watch was also under pressure from Mortar and machine gun fire. They had been joined by Lieutenant Colonel Honeyman, who had been thwarted in his attempt to return to Battalion Headquarters by enemy armoured cars blocking the road. At daybreak on 12 June three companies were still holding their own and with a battery from 23/Field Regiment and a platoon from the 1/Kensingtons protecting them, they realised they had missed the embarkation deadline, unaware that the troops on either flank had already left. They fought on, vastly outnumbered by the men of 5th Panzer Division and the 2nd Motorized Division; but by noon Honeyman realized it was all over, particularly as a detachment of French cavalrymen that were fighting near to them had just surrendered. Nearby was Second Lieutenant Angus Irwin, whose carrier platoon had rescued the wounded from the perimeter. According to Irwin, the last attack by the enemy went a long way to change Honeyman's mind:

As the final attack was coming in, Colonel Honeyman was standing near me and said, 'I never thought this would happen. Certainly not that I would ever have to chuck the can in, but I'm afraid we are going to have to give up to save lives because we're completely surrounded.' He then sent some runners to give the order to cease fire.

Honeyman himself documented the last hour of the enemy attack:

The Germans attack opened at 0700 hrs, after a night of rain, with heavy shelling and mortar fire. Our Forward Observation Officer reported the line to the guns broken (the guns had, unknown to us, been destroyed). Gradually tanks encircled the locality and infantry infiltration progressed. This portion of the Battalion suffered severe casualties and eventually even small arms ammunition ran out. We had no A/T guns and Lieut. Alastair Telfer-Smollett was killed. About 1100 hrs Captain Grant Duff was killed at the head of his Coy, leading it from one position to another in an endeavour to beat off the German attack. About 1200 hrs the Chasseurs Alpins forestalled the CO by deciding to capitulate; in fact, further resistance was only causing needless loss of life, and food, water, and ammunition were all exhausted. Withdrawal across open country was out of the question and gallant efforts of the Carrier Platoon under Lieutenant Irwin to evacuate casualties met with no success. German tanks were all around us. Casualties in these two days were estimated at about fifty killed and 200 wounded.

19-year-old Second Lieutenant Alastair Telfer-Smollett and 29-year-old Captain Neill Grant Duff are both buried in Houdetot Churchyard Cemetery.

St Valery-en-Caux

Once the western perimeter had been breached by tanks, Fortune was left with a tactical dilemma. German tanks and artillery now occupied a position on the western cliffs overlooking the town and harbour as well as the evacuation beaches. An inner perimeter line had been established and was manned by the survivors of four companies of 7/Norfolks and associated machine gunners (they would be reinforced by one company from each unit as it withdrew). French troops were supposed to guard the western cliffs, but few had arrived, and those that did hurriedly withdrew in the face of German tanks. The western edge of the line was soon threatened by German tanks. Major Ellis, the author of the Official History volume *The War in France and Flanders*, drew attention to General Fortune's dilemma :

In spite of all efforts the infiltration of St Valery was hard to prevent, as the German artillery and machine guns on the cliff tops maintained a continuous fire on the town and beaches. Small parties of 1/Kensingtons and 7/Royal Northumberland Fusiliers (both machine gun battalions) and the 7/Norfolks (pioneers) succeeded in pushing the enemy back to the wooded outskirts of the town, but the position in St Valery was now very grave. The enemy's capture of the western cliffs threatened the whole embarkation plan, for the cliffs were within the inner perimeter on which the final stand was intended and some of the planned embarkation points were now under close range enemy artillery and machine-gun fire.

Nevertheless, Fortune was determined to proceed with the evacuation so much so that an order was given to all divisional troops that evacuation would begin at 10.30 that night.

The Evacuation
The fleet lying offshore on 11 June consisted of sixty-seven merchant ships and about 140 smaller vessels and warships. During the morning the ships close to shore had come under fire from an enemy battery on the western cliffs and as a result had been ordered to sea immediately. By the afternoon the whole rescue fleet was spread out 7 miles north-west of St Valery-en-Caux, but by then it was too late; fog had come down, obscuring the coast from view. The tug *Fair Play* landed beach parties on 12 June at a place slightly west of St Valery-en-Caux, but heavy fire was opened by the enemy and four of their boats were destroyed. The sloop *Hebe II* took off eighty men from the beach close to the town but she was sunk and her commanding officer killed. Offshore it was reported that a naval tow of four or five boats had also been sunk by enemy gunfire and after that no other boats had come in. The failure of the evacuation attempts on 12 June was mitigated somewhat by the news that Second Lieutenant Walker of the 7/Norfolks, and eighteen men had commandeered a fishing boat on the western beach and were eventually picked up at sea by HMS *Harvester*.

The troops on the outer perimeter had orders to report to the railway station in the town, where they would get further instructions; unfortunately no-one was there in authority. Major (Prince) Alphonse de Chimay of the 1/Kensingtons was one officer who turned up at the railway station:

> When we got to the station there was no sign of any guides and there were great numbers of troops practically crowded shoulder to shoulder. There was no shelling near the station and I therefore decided to leave the company there and go forward to see if I could get any news of the evacuation.

HMS *Harvester*.

The railway station at St Valery-en-Caux was destroyed in early 1945.

We will hear more of de Chimay later in the chapter. The streets at this time were full of soldiers from practically every unit in the division, lit up by the blazing houses. Fortunately the inner perimeter still held, preventing the bulk of the Germans from penetrating the town. At midnight a destroyer and two sloops were spotted by the troops onshore and a few troops managed to clamber aboard before the enemy appeared along the beach from the west and forced the landing boats to withdraw. It became obvious to all concerned that there was no hope of evacuation from St Valery.

Veules-les-Roses

Veules-les-Roses is a small town about 4 miles east of St Valery-en-Caux. One of the tragic events of the day was the fact that at Veulesles-Roses a large number of British soldiers were being embarked. Had the bulk of the 51st Division known of this a great many men could have marched along the beach and got away. The first ship to reach Veules on 12 June was the SS *Goldfinch,* who began using her lifeboats to ferry soldiers back to the ship. She was joined by two destroyers, HMS *Saladin* and HMS *Codrington,* and the Dutch Scuyt *Pascholl.* Lieutenant Thompson, the commander of the *Goldfinch*, expressed his admiration for the men his boats had picked up from the beach:

> It was a revelation to see men, who had been waiting for days without proper food or rest, helping to pull the boats out to the ship. Most of them were exhausted when they came aboard, Many were wounded.

113

SS *Goldfinch* rescued more than 400 men. She had been joined in her work by such ships as the SS *Guernsey Queen* and the drifter SS *Golden Harvest*; much of the praise for this achievement should go to Commander Chatwin and Sub-Lieutenants Killam and McLernon, who were part of the beach party landed by HMS *Codrington*. They alone ensured discipline in the queues that formed, boats consequently leaving before they were fully loaded.

Although there was intermittent fire during the early morning, a heavy bombardment that opened up at 8.30am against the boats on the beach prompted all the British boats to leave. As they left the beach *Pascholl* reported that many French soldiers were left on the beach. A total of 1,300 British and 900 French troops were taken off from Veules-les-Roses on the morning of 12 June; bearing in mind that Fortune had hoped to evacuate 24,000 men, it was an insignificant number.

Major de Chimay could find no trace of any ships at St Valery and reported men were using various signals by lamp to attract their attention. There was no fog but smoke from the burning buildings was drifting out to sea. Lieutenant Colonel (acting Brigadier) Barclay was most concerned about the men on the jetty and thought when daylight came heavy casualties would be incurred and the wounded hit. He asked de Chimay to assist in getting some of the men away, which he did, noting about 200 troops followed him along the sea front:

> I then carried on along the shore and eventually I rounded a corner and saw the boats, some 4 miles away at Veules-les-Roses. The cliff is about 300 feet (high) most of the way between St Valery and Veules-les-Roses and many of the men who tried to get down had been killed in so doing. I estimate the number at about fifty. Some were tying rifle slings together in order to get down. When I reached the boast there were a considerable number of French troops who were mobbing any small boat that came in reach, and at least one was beached as a result. I managed to wade out to a whaler and asked to see the senior Naval Officer, who I informed of the position at St Valery and that a considerable number of men were there. I was then taken on [board] the *Duke of York* and shortly on reaching it the shelling started again and the fleet had to move out. It must have been about 5.00am.

De Chimay mentioned that they left a number of the smaller boats and that considerable numbers of men were running along the cliff tops and descending on ropes at Veules-les-Roses. On board the *Duke of York* were 206 British troops with eleven officers and 126 French troops with two officers. There were some sixteen casualties who were being cared for by Captain James Sugden of the Duke of Wellington's. De Chimay had not intended to leave Veules-les-Roses on the *Duke of York* but merely wanted to alert the Navy to the possibility that even more men were waiting at St Valery. But it was too late; de Chimay was on his way to England.

The cliffs at Veules-les-Roses

Lieutenant Roger Sandford, the Intelligence Officer of the 1/Black Watch, was also at Veules-les-Roses, having descended the cliffs on a rope. He wrote of his experiences:

As far as I could see, the French were still holding the perimeter to the west of St Valery and as evening came they surrendered to the Germans and allowed the German light tanks and armoured fighting vehicles to cut our defence in half. Then Brigadier Burney and staff, according to PSM Clarke, left for St Valery about 10.00pm. How we never got the message to retire before 12.20am will some day be told maybe ...

When I got to the crest the whole cliff top was alive with Frenchman trying to get down the cliff. There was not a single break from St Valery to Veules-les-Roses for about 7 miles. To the north east the average height was about 300 feet or a little more. When I eventually got down on car tow ropes tied together there were about ninety Frenchmen to every ten English on the beach. There was a summer mist on the sea and no lifeboats had come in as they could not tell what was happening. The mist soon lifted and after signals they towed lifeboats in with naval pinnaces. As the lifeboats touched the beach all the French panicked and made a dive for the boats in front of the wounded. They broke up three and made them unseaworthy.

115

A second lieutenant in the Dukes Regiment, who had quite a lot of men with him, fixed bayonets and drove the French up the beach, killing a colonel and about fifty others. Major de Chimay, from the 1/Kensingtons, of all people suddenly turned up. He was the machine-gun company commander (sic) and we got grenades to hold the French off until all the wounded were shipped off. Finally we both swam and were hauled in At this point Lang must have been aware of the pinnace. We begged the Navy to hang on but at about 6.15pm they (the Germans) started shelling with A/T guns and three [shells] went straight though one boat and bounced acrosss the water until it sank. We then, to our sorrow, had to weigh anchor and get out while the going was still good.

As the evacuation ended at Veules-les-Roses and discipline vanished into thin air, Fortune was still determined to do anything possible to hang on for another day to give the Navy one more chance to take the Division off. Unbeknown to Fortune, most of the ships had already gone, so even if it would have been possible to extend the defence of St Valery for another day, the chances of ships being on hand to embark troops were small. General Fortune was not to know this and set about planning the defence of the town.

Apart from the men of the 2/7 Duke of Wellington's, the only other unit to escape largely intact were the territorials of 385/Battery of the 1/Royal Horse Artillery. Commanded by 31-year-old Major William Mullens, the battery remained in position until 4.00pm. Finding no ships at St Valery, the Major led his men to Veules-les-Roses and, consequently, 160 men of the battery escaped.

The Final Hours
Second Lieutenant RegWood of the 1/Kensingtons, who was soon to be captured, recorded the final hours of the garrison at St Valery-en-Caux in his diary:

To add to our discomfort and misery, it had now stated raining ... An enemy attack was launched again in the perimeter but was beaten off, chiefly due to the 25-pounders, who fired their last rounds. Soon after-wards enemy bombers came over and the quay hospital and some MTBs were hit. Meanwhile, the French corps commander (Ihler) has twice hoisted the white flag on the chateau a mile away and both times it was shot down by British troops ...

Unfortunately every unit left at St Valery had practically run out of ammunition and there was only enough for about ten minutes firing, there was no food and precious little water. The enemy were obviously massing for a large scale attack and there was no hope of holding then off with our depleted ammunition. We should be at the mercy of the bombers, as the Bofors guns had no ammunition at all. The French

This photograph, which appeared in the German magazine *Signal*, shows British soldiers being led into captivity at Veules-les-Roses. Colin Hunter is in the centre right of the picture with a bandaged eye; Derek Lang is shown on the extreme right.

were either packing in everywhere or deserting and so in all these circumstances, and to avoid unnecessary waste of life, General Fortune decided to surrender at 8.00am.

Enemy infantry were now in force along the beaches and, as we had expended the last of our ammunition, we destroyed the guns and scattered the locks. I burnt all my papers and soon after came the

German tanks descend into St Valery-en-Caux.

By the end of the battle some 70 per cent of the town had been destroyed.

The well known photograph of General Fortune standing with Erwin Rommel outside the former Hotel de Ville at Valery-en-Caux. Fortune was one of the most senior British officers to be captured during the war.

order to cease all further resistance. As we left to go back to Company HQ we were overtaken by enemy tanks. An officer, who spoke excellent English, relieved me of my pistol.

Some units did hold out for some time and troops of the 1/Black Watch at Houdetot did not surrender until several hours after the Division; the same applied to units of the 2/Seaforths and 1/Gordons. Various accounts exist of the emotion felt by members of the infantry. Many regarded it as a total humiliation and for all there was shock and disbelief; but none is perhaps more poignant than the account by Colour Sergeant Gregor Macdonald of the 4/Cameron Highlanders:

> To say we were shocked would be an understatement. As infantry soldiers we had at some time imagined ourselves wounded or even killed but now our only thought was the humiliation of the Highland Division surrendering.

It is a feeling that remains in Scotland today.

Cemeteries Visited
Apart from those described in Chapter 10, we visited one other, at **Manneville-es-Plains**. Here the small cemetery is contained within the churchyard and the visitor will find the headstones amongst the civilian

119

The entrance to the church at Manneville-es-Plains.

graves. The church can be found on **Rue du Manoir** and there is car parking almost opposite. A short walk along the Rue du Manoir will take you into the churchyard, where the six headstones will become immediately apparent. The majority of those buried here are from the 5/Gordons and may have been killed on the way back from St-Pierre-le-Viger.

Chapter 9

Conclusions

After the surrender, the defiant figure of General Fortune was directed to the quayside, where a group of generals that included Rommel, Ihler and a collection of divisional commanders had gathered. After formally accepting Fortune's surrender, Rommel invited General Fortune for lunch and, although desperately hungry, Fortune declined the invitation, saying lunch had been already been prepared for him. It was a blatant untruth that he would later regret, but this stubbornness was a character trait and he felt he had to do something. Rommel allowed him, and other commanders, to keep their batmen as a token of respect.

Fortune spent the rest of the war as a prisoner of war. As a senior British officer in captivity in Germany, he worked to improve the conditions of the men under his command. He suffered a stroke in 1944 but refused repatriation. He was liberated in April 1945 and made KBE shortly after. He died in 1949.

It is intriguing to note that Marshall-Cornwall, the liaison officer with the French Tenth Army, contacted the War Office on 8 June to express his fear that the 51st Division was in danger of being cut off and that he (Marshall-Cornwall) had completely lost faith in the French ability to stand firm against the enemy. The contents of this message was too much of a sensitive issue for the War Office to deal with; but there is little doubt that the crucial cause of almost all of the 51st Division's troubles can be traced back to it being under an ineffectual French command.

Robert Gardner is of the opinion that, as it was unfeasible for the Division to return to the BEF, it could be argued that instead of being re-directed to the Somme the Division could possibly have been sent to Rouen. There it would have joined forced with the Beauman Division and the 1st Armoured Division to create a British corps of two infantry divisions and one much reduced armoured division. Gardner feels that this force could have worked with the French IX Corps to hold the line of the Seine until the second BEF arrived in early June. The author is of a mind to agree with him.

It was always planned for the 51st Division to join the second BEF, that is, if Sir John Dill, who was Chief of the Imperial General Staff at the time, was to be taken at his word! It was certainly in Britain's best interests if a second BEF were to be formed and that it be reinforced by a battle hardened and strong division. What transpired instead was a division that was placed in a very difficult position and kept under the command of the French, whose spirit and whose ability to fight was effectively non-existent

Sir John Dill became CIGS after Sir Edmund Ironside. He died in Washington when head of the British Military Mission; his grave is one of only two in Arlington marked by a figure mounted on a horse.

and who were severely weakened by past events on the Meuse at Sedan. However, there was little movement on the part of the War Office to redress the situation and it is a charge of negligence that should be levelled at the British government rather than one of premeditated sacrifice by Churchill.

For those who were lucky enough to get away from Veules-les-Roses and St Valery-en-Caux, the journey home would have been a high point in their minds; but for those who were captured they paid the very heavy price of five years in prisoner of war camps. More than 10,000 men were taken prisoner at St Valery, and with the 1,000 taken prisoner on the Somme and Saar, over 11,000 soldiers of the Division marched into captivity. The column marched some 16 miles per day to the railhead at Hulst in the Netherlands and during this time food was virtually non-existent, leaving the prisoners to steal from nearby fields or to survive from handouts from French and Belgian civilians. It is difficult to imagine how men forced to march long distances each day on starvation rations often managed to stay alert; but many did and it remains one of the lasting tributes to many of the captured men of the Division that they continued in their efforts to escape from the column.

Escapes

A large number of soldiers from all units of the Division made daring escape attempts from the marching column as it wound its way to the rail-

A column of French prisoners being marched into captivity.

head. Some were recaptured almost immediately, some were shot as they ran for cover, but others managed to get back to England after months of evading capture by the Germans and Vichy French. By the end of June 1941, 290 British prisoners of war had returned to Britain; 134 of these men were members of the 51st Division.

Many of the British soldiers that arrived at Veules-les-Roses were too late to be rescued. One of these men was Captain Derek Lang, the Adjutant of the 4/Camerons. He and Brigadier Barclay then headed for Veules-les-Roses. Lang eventually reached two boats, the larger was a French ship and the smaller was a British fishing; boat but both boats looked crowded and, to cap it all, both had run aground and were unable to move. As German artillery opened up from the cliff tops, Lang was horrified to see the boats demolished before his eyes. He made reference to it in his book *Return to St Valery*:

The big guns on the cliffs near St Valery opened up on the Frenchman. Bravely she replied with her 3-pounder but the shells could scarcely have got half way to the target. It was not long before the German guns found the exact range and then we had a ringside seat at this macabre play, watching in horror as they systematically destroyed the crowded ship. It must have been hit a dozen times before the little gun was finally silenced and a few minutes later the riddled hulk slid over on its side.

Lang had probably watched the demise of the French ship *Cerons*. The German guns then turned their attention to the British boat and Lang was struck on the forehead by shrapnel, losing consciousness.

Whether Lang was aware of Major de Chimay will probably never be known but, as they were both on the beach at the same time, it is likely. By early afternoon nearly all the survivors from the two boats had been taken prisoner and the remainder were rounded up later. But luck favours the brave and Lang escaped from Tournai on his second attempt in July, making his way to Palestine and Jerusalem and eventually arriving in England in 1942, where he took up an appointment at the School of Infantry. Later, in 1944, he became commanding officer of the 5/Cameron Highlanders, a battalion that he joined while they were still at the invasion bridgehead. The battalion was a TA unit formed in 1939 as a second line duplicate of the 4/Battalion and now formed part of the 152nd Brigade of Major General 'Tom' Rennie's reconstituted 51st (Highland) Division. Rennie himself was an escaper from St Valery-en-Caux.

The Germans vacated St Valery two days before the arrival of the 51st Division on its return to France in 1944; its triumphal entry into the town was to do largely with Montgomery. It was his wish that the Division should recapture St Valéry and he asked the Canadian Army commander to arrange this. Rennie was killed during *Operation Plunder*, the Allied crossing of the River Rhine, in March 1945. Macintosh-Walker became a brigadier and was killed during the battle of Normandy in June 1944.

(*Left*) Derek Lang in a contemporary photograph. (*Right*) General Bernard Montgomery.

124

Major General 'Tom' Rennie.

Of the 1/Kensingtons who escaped, we already know of Major de Chimay's evacuation. Several more men escaped by boat, including CSM Satchwell and a party of eight, who escaped from St Valery, arriving in England on 13 June. Private Ford of the 1/Kensingtons was another man who escaped from the marching column of prisoners and returned to England several months later, on 4 December. Privates Hugh Oliver and Neill Cambell of the 4/Camerons also escaped the column, on the pretence of getting water, reaching the coast after walking for three days. Spotting a likely twenty foot sailing boat at St Valery-en-Caux they eventually worked their way through an opening between the gates and the wall of the inner harbour. They were picked up by HMS *Dalmatia* and finally landed at Portsmouth on 7 July.

Commander Elkins, the naval officer, who had been put ashore to 'keep an eye' on the Division, and Captain Leslie Hulls, the 153 Brigade Intelligence Officer, escaped from a prisoner of war transit camp near Breteuil after three days of marching in the column. Using Hull's knowledge of French and Elkin's pocket compass, the pair made their way to the Atlantic coast and finally managed to steal an 18-foot fishing boat at Lion-sur-Mer, arriving near Portsmouth on 25 June. Hull is reputed to be the only British officer to have escaped from captivity in both world wars.

Captain 'Bill' Bradford, the Adjutant of the 1/Black Watch, escaped from the prisoner of war column on 19 June. Travelling by bicycle he

125

reached the Pyrenees in July but was arrested by the Vichy French when he tried to cross into Spain. From there he was taken to the notorious Montferran Concentration camp until he was transferred to Fort St Jean in Marseilles. He managed to get away from there and eventually stowed away on a ship bound for Algiers. Following a period of illness he was approached by a man who had bought a 17-foot sailing yacht and was asked if he would help him sail the boat to Gibraltar. After a week-long voyage, covering nearly 700 miles, the boat was spotted by a Royal Navy patrol ship, the *Sayonara*. Bradford was finally able to leave Gibraltar and arrived in Glasgow on 11 July 1941. He later joined the 5/Black Watch and commanded the Battalion from July 1944. He retired as a Brigadier.

A remarkable escape was made by two pairs of men who escaped on 12 June. All four escaped from their marching columns of prisoners – probably the same column – at or near Forges-les-Eaux. From that point on they overtook, and then kept ahead of, the main German forces travelling west. RQMS Griffiths and Driver Baker wore civilian clothes found in abandoned buildings, rode on stolen bicycles and made their way to Caen which, although occupied, had a refugee centre, where they picked up news of the latest German advances. They reached the coast at Granville on 23 June, where they were guided to a boat on which they spent the night before setting out early next morning to reach the Isles of Chausey at about midday.

Driver Johnson and Driver Day, both Royal Engineers, tell much the same story and describe joining a small party and boarding a fishing smack from Granville, which sailed at two in the morning for Chausey. Neither of the pairs of men mention the other but their stories are so similar from this point (although their dates do not match exactly) that it is reasonable to suppose they may have travelled together. From Chausey, Johnson and Day boarded a small pleasure steamer, which left at 3 o'clock that afternoon for Jersey, where all four men were accommodated at the Royal Yacht Hotel in St Helier before catching the evening's overnight Southern Railway mail steamer to Southampton.

Company Quartermaster Sergeant Macdonald and Private John Mac-Glynn of the 4/Camerons escaped from the line of march on 18 June. Recaptured near Amiens, they escaped again from a farm where the Germans were holding them and jumped a train, before crossing France on foot. Although Macdonald parted company from MacGlynn (he found out later that MacGlynn had arrived back at home safely), Macdonald's route took him to Marseilles, from where he was guided over the Pyrenees into Spain. After a few more adventures his release was finally secured by the British Embassy from one of Franco's prisons and on 23 February 1941 he arrived in Glasgow.

For those who were unable or unwilling to escape from the column, 12 June was the beginning of five years of captivity. Escaping from a prisoner of war camp was one thing but getting home safely to Britain was

A fishing smack similar to the one used by Drivers Johnson and Day.

quite another. One man who succeeded in both was Second Lieutenant Blair of the 2/Seaforths. He escaped from a working party in southern Germany and took eight days to walk to Switzerland, a distance of some 75 miles. At Berne, the British Military Attaché (himself a successful Great War escaper) provided him with money and he went from there to Madrid. Before the month was out he was back at home, the first Army officer to make it out of a prisoner of war camp. He ended life as a lieutenant general and with a knighthood. Blair obviously started something, as Second Lieutenant Peter Douglas of the 8/Argylls escaped the day after Blair and Second Lieutenant Angus Rowan-Hamilton of the 1/Black Watch escaped ten weeks later.

One of the most remarkable escapes from St Valery-en-Caux was led by the only unwounded officer of the 2/Seaforths. Walking by night and hiding by day, Second Lieutenant Richard Broad and his men reached the Seine at Duclair on 19 June, crossing the river the following day in a boat lent by a local schoolmaster. Helped by numerous other sympathisers, including the English Mother Superior of the convent at Honfleur and the Prefect of Police in Calvados, who was also head of the fledgling resistance, the men were hidden until February 1941, when they were moved to Marseilles via Paris.

Within days seven of the men had been arrested by the Vichy authorities and were sent to the notorious Fort St Hyppolyte, near Nimes. Broad, who

Second Lieutenant Richard Broad.

had evaded capture, soon managed to wangle the release of six of them; Private Osborne, who had been wounded by German sentries while crossing the line between Occupied and Vichy France, had to be left in hospital. The remaining seven crossed the Spanish frontier on 16 February only to be arrested again on arrival in Barcelona by Spanish Police. After languishing for two months in Franco's notorious political prisons, they too were released with the assistance of the British Embassy in Madrid. Two weeks later they were repatriated by boat via Gibraltar, arriving in Liverpool on 15 May1941. Thanks largely to Richard Broad's determination and resource, 'Snow White and the Seven Dwarfs', as they were known by the French resistance, were the single largest group from the Highland Division to return home through France and Spain.

It was not only those men who were captured at St Valery-en-Caux and Veules-les-Roses that managed to get home. Corporal A. MacDonald, Lance Corporal J. Wilson and Private W. Kemp were taken prisoner near Abbeville on 7 June. MacDonald and Wilson had already served ten years in the Territorials whilst Kemp had been a peacetime policeman. All three were serving with C Company of 8/Argyll & Sutherland Highlanders when their unit was captured near Vignacourt. They were first driven to join another 500 British and 5,000 French prisoners of war and then marched across country. On 14 June, as they approached Cambrin, east of Béthune, they slipped from the column to begin their long trek south. The first priority was to get some civilian clothes and these were soon supplied by a young French boy, who produced 'workmen's blue' trousers and blouses, plus berets and a haversack for each man. With this disguise the three men decided to travel by day and rest by night, both to aid navigation and to avoid the problems of the newly imposed curfew.

On their travels they encountered German soldiers but each time were able to convince them that they were Belgian refugees, a story reinforced when they acquired a perambulator which they filled with discarded pots and pans and pushed ahead of them. Reaching Aumale on 21 June, they found three bicycles in an abandoned cycle shop that speeded up their progress until they were arrested by German troops and taken to join 3,000 French prisoners. They tried sticking to their story of being Belgian until interrogated by a French speaking German officer who couldn't understand a word of their Gaelic. When he finally produced an atlas, Kemp took the initiative, pointed to the Ukraine and somehow managed to convey the idea that they were Russians, a story they were to use several more times in their travels.

Continuing on foot once more, they were heading for Vihiers when they stopped a bus and tried a new tactic. Posing as Americans in the French Foreign Legion they convinced the driver to take them to Niort. From there they hitch-hiked to Bordeaux and, arriving on 4 July, decided it was a good day to visit the American Consulate. Unfortunately the Consul declined to help them. They continued south, where they repeated their story of being American Legionnaires at a mairie, but the mayor was no help either. They finally reached Bayonne on 10 July. With the help of a French sergeant, Roger Panetta, they made their first crossing into Spain, where they were promptly arrested by a Spanish soldier who had them escorted back to France that night.

At 6.00am they tried again but were caught once more the following morning and again returned to France. However one of the Spanish officers told them of a better route to try next time, which would avoid the border guards and take them to San Sebastian. They set off late the next day only to get themselves lost and find themselves back in France yet again. Finally, they and Panetta swam across the Bidassoa River and walked to San Sebastian, arriving on 15 July, where they were directed to the British Consulate. They arrived back in Glasgow on 28 July 1940.

Not all 'escapers' had to climb over the wire or evade a PoW marching column from St Valery to get home. Lieutenant Colonel Ansell, who was blinded by the Gordons in a friendly fire incident, was eventually repatriated in 1942 after a long, involved process and was told that more

Lieutenant Colonel Mike Ansell in captivity. Ansell is the tall figure, second from the left in the photograph.

operations on his eyes would be to no avail. Despite his handicap he was invited to take up the position of chairman of the British Show Jumping Association; he has been credited with revitalizing the sport. He restarted the Royal International Horse Show and initiated the Horse of the Year Show. He was Chairman of the British Horse Society and chaired the British Show Jumping Association from 1945 until 1964. He was the first president of the British Equestrian Federation. He died in February 1994.

Finale

On 2 September 1944 the reformed 51st (Highland) Division marched into St Valery-en-Caux. At the head of the lead battalion was Lieutenant Colonel Derek Lang, commanding the 5/Camerons; also present was Lieutenant Colonel 'Bill' Bradford, who commanded the 5/Black Watch. They laid the wreath at the memorial service for the men who had died in 1940. During the advance on St Valery-en-Caux, Major General 'Tom' Rennie reminded the Division of the fate that befell the original Highland Division;

> True to the highland tradition it remained to the last with the remnants of our French Allies, although it was within its capacity to withdraw and embark at Le Havre ... It has been our task to avenge the fate of out less fortunate comrades and that we have nearly accomplished ... We have lived up to the great traditions of the 51st and of Scotland.

Lieutenant Colonel Bradford, CO of the 5/Black Watch, laying a wreath at the cemetery in St Valery-en-Caux on 2 September 1944.

The last words, attributed to Major Lionel Ellis, the official Historian of the France and Flanders Campaign of 1940, give much room for thought:

Withdrawal is a valid operation of war: ability to withdraw when occasion warrants it is often a prelude to eventual victory. But a long fighting withdrawal is also one of the most difficult operations of war, for it taxes severely the moral and physical strength of the troops and the skill and steady courage of their commanders.

Chapter 10

The Tours

General Advice to Battlefield Tourists
There are several opportunities for the battlefield visitor to stretch their legs during the tours. There are short walks/drives: one in Franleu, where there is a walk/drive, another in Huppy and one other in St Pierre-le-Viger. A further walk/drive is in St Valery-en-Caux. The author strongly suggests obtaining maps from the various Tourist Offices along the route to supplement your excursions and taking the time to prepare at home before you arrive. While much of the area covered by the guide is dotted with cafés and other refreshment venues, it is always wise to have something to eat and drink with you.

Maps
The tours described in this book are best supported by the IGN Série Bleu 1:25000 maps, which can be purchased at most good tourist offices, the bigger local supermarkets and online from www.mapsworldwide.com. The area of St Valery-en-Caux, as described in the text, is contained within the Carte de Randonnée 1909 OT. Visitors may also wish to purchase the Carte de Randonnée 1809 OT Fécamp, which gives some insight into the area south, towards Le Havre. Franleu is marked on the Carte de Randonnée 2107 OT.

Bear in mind that satellite navigation can be a very useful supplement in supporting general route finding, particularly when trying to locate obscure CWGC cemeteries; and it is always useful to use the street view on Google Earth prior to any visit. The CWGC App for your phone is also of great use and the author has used it prior to visiting the area and again while trying to locate obscure cemeteries in Normandy.

Travel and Where to Stay
By far the quickest passage across the Channel is via the Tunnel at Folkstone, the thirty-six minutes travelling time comparing favourably with the longer ferry journey from Dover to Calais or Dunkerque. However, it is worth considering Calais to Le Havre and Newhaven to Dieppe, which is a longer ferry journey but only a short distance to drive. Whether your choice of route is over or under the Channel, early booking is always recommended if advantage is to be taken of the cheaper fares. Travelling times vary according to traffic; but as a rough guide the journey from Calais to Franleu is 74 miles via the A16, a drive of about one and a half hours. Calais to St Valery en Caux is about two and a half hours and roughly the same distance via the A16 – provided the excursion to Franleu

and Huppy are avoided! Newhaven to Dieppe is much shorter by road, as is Le Havre.

Accomodation

With regard to accommodation, you have the choice of staying locally on the coast at St Valery-en-Caux, Veuleles-Roses or further afield at Dieppe. Dieppe has some of the more well known chain hotels but there is plenty of good self catering and B&B accommodation in the area. The **Hotel De La Terrace** at Varengeville-sur-Mer, near Dieppe, can be personally recommended and offers good quality accommodation, free WiFi, parking and an excellent restaurant. The three-stars **Hotel Casino** in St Valery-en-Caux is also of good quality, but make sure you book early to avoid disappointment. Further afield at Étoutteville is the **Hotel L'Hirondelle**, which is also of good quality. There are numerous apartments in both St Valery-en-Caux and the neighbouring towns of Veules-les-Roses, Manneville-des-Plains and Neville, details of which can be found on the internet.

For those who prefer the outdoor life there is a profusion of campsites along this section of the coast. A mobile home park is at 18 Avenue Foch in St Valery-en-Caux; while on Avenue du Ham is **Camping d'Etennemare**, which boasts a pool as well as mobile homes for rent and tents. Further information on all aspects of accommodation can be obtained from the various Tourist Offices in the main centres at St Valery-en-Caux, Veules-les-Roses and Dieppe. All locations described in the text were correct at the time of publication.

The Hotel De La Terrace at Varengeville-sur-Mer.

Driving

Driving abroad is not the expedition it was years ago and most battlefield visitors may well have already made the journey several times. However, if this is the first time you have ventured on French roads there are one or two common sense rules to take into consideration. Ensure your vehicle is properly insured and covered by suitable breakdown insurance; if in doubt contact your insurer, who will advise you. There are also a number of compulsory items to be carried by motorists that are required by French law. These include your driving licence and vehicle registration documents, a warning triangle, a Conformité Européenne (CE) approved fluorescent safety vest for each person travelling in the car, headlamp beam convertors and the visible display of a UK sticker. Even if not a requirement by now, it is advisable to have a green card for your insurance. Whereas some modern cars have built in headlight convertors and many have a UK plate incorporated into the rear number plate, it is still law to have a separate UK sticker. French law also requires the vehicle to be equipped with a first aid kit and, if not now, possibly sooner or later, a breath test kit. If you fail to have these available there are some hefty on the spot fines for these motoring offences if caught driving without them. Most, if not all, of these items can be purchased at the various outlets at the Tunnel, the Channel port at Dover and on board the ferries themselves. There is no shop on the trains. On a more personal note it is always advisable to take out personal accident insurance and a reserve supply of any medication that you may be taking at the time may also be useful. Here are three tips that the author has always found useful when driving:

1. When driving on single carriageway roads try to stop at petrol stations on the right hand side of the road. It is much more natural then to continue driving on the right hand side of the road after you leave. Leaving a garage or supermarket is often the time when you find yourself naturally turning onto the wrong side of the road. Garages are often unmanned and require you to pay at the pump with your credit card – so be warned when you fill up.

2. Take your time! Don't rush! If you rush your instinct may take over and your instinct is geared to driving on the left and, remember, indicators are often not used and the direction some vehicles are intending to take can be difficult to determine.

3. Pay particular care on roundabouts. A lot of drivers do not, or rarely appear to, use indicators. Navigators, remember to look at the signs anti-clockwise and drivers remember that the danger is coming from the left.

Visiting Commonwealth War Graves Commission Cemeteries

The CWGC cemeteries visited in this guide are often to be found in communal cemeteries, such as Mons-Boubert Communal Cemetery, although you will find British casualties from 1940 located in a number of existing

First World War Cemeteries, such as Abbeville Communal Cemetery Extension. There are very few exclusive war cemeteries, such as Grandcourt War Cemetery. Headstones from the composite and attached units of the 51st Division can be found in communal cemeteries from Abbeville to St Valery-en-Caux and beyond and is indicative of the length of their withdrawal and the strength of the German forces that were following them. Visitors should also remember that where a soldier has been recovered from the battlefield it was not always possible to identify exactly when he was killed or died. To that end, on some headstones the CWGC has provided two dates, between which, it is presumed, the individual died.

When visiting the fallen from the Second World War in the area, it is possible that you will be reminded of casualties from the First World War, the numbers of which probably horrified the men of the BEF who fought in this area during June 1940. The visitor will also come across the graves of aircrew that were shot down over the course of the war and those men who died during the 1944 advance after the D-Day landings. The graves of men killed in the area during June 1940 are probably some of the least visited in the whole of Northern France, especially since the 51st Division was engaged in numerous small actions; we should visit these graves where possible to pay our respects. These small numbers of men, whose headstones are sometimes lost amongst the myriad of French civilian graves in communal cemeteries, are often all but forgotten.

The Imperial (since the early 1960s, the 'Commonwealth') War Graves Commission, was responsible for introducing the standardised headstone,

Abbeville Communal Cemetery Extension.

Grandcourt War Cemetery.

which brought equality in death regardless of rank, race or creed, and it is this familiar white headstone that you will see now in all CWGC cemeteries. Keep an eye open for the green and white directional signs. Where there is a CWGC plot within a communal or churchyard cemetery, the familiar green and white sign at the entrance with the words Tombes [or 'Tombe' if only one CWGC casualty is buried there] de Guerre du Commonwealth will indicate their presence. French military cemeteries are usually marked by the French national flag, whilst those that are contained within communal cemeteries are often marked by a sign at the cemetery entrance bearing the words: *Carré Militaire, Tombes de Soldats, Morts pour la France.*

The green and white sign, usually at the entrance to the cemetery, that indicate the presence of Commonwealth War Graves.

137

Walk 1: Franleu

The 7/Argyll and Sutherland Highlanders were embodied on 1 September 1939 and two days later the Second World War began. A month after the declaration of war the Battalion bade Stirling good-bye and entrained for Aldershot. Leaving Scotland was a big event in the lives of the young soldiers, many of whom had not been far from their homes before.

Shortly afterwards the advanced party set off for France and on 12 February 1940 the remainder of the Battalion boarded the SS *Fenella* at Southampton and sailed for Le Havre. On 31 May the Battalion took over a section of the front in Normandy from a French cavalry Regiment, the 11/Cuirassiers. In May/June 154 Brigade was on the left of the Divisional front and was responsible for the sector that ran for 8 miles from the coast, just south of Abbeville. In the Battalion's sector there were a number of small villages and the defensive plan was based around them.

The position on 1 June was relatively simple. Franleu was the designated village in which Battalion Headquarters of the 7/Argyll and Sutherland Highlanders were located, and was held by Headquarters Company. The remaining men of the battalion were holding the surrounding villages: B Company held Saigneville, C Company held Mons-Boubert, while

The rear of the school building that was Battalion Headquarters of the 7/Argylls at Franleu, taken from the orchard.

D Company held Cattigny and Arrest. A Company were in reserve at Quesnoy-le-Montant. On 4 June the Highland Division and the French had launched an attack on Abbeville which failed and by nightfall the enemy had regained its positions from where they launched *Fall Rot* the next day on 5 June. The battalion was not in a position to conduct a co-ordinated fight against the advancing Germans, largely because the positions were too scattered and thus the battle developed into a series of isolated actions, with each company hold its own area until they were overwhelmed.

This walk takes place from the schoolhouse at Franleu, where **Lieutenant Colonel Buchanan** and his men held out for two days, north to Mons-Boubert to visit the graves of Private Henderson and an unnamed soldier

A modern map of Franleu, showing the details of the walk/drive.

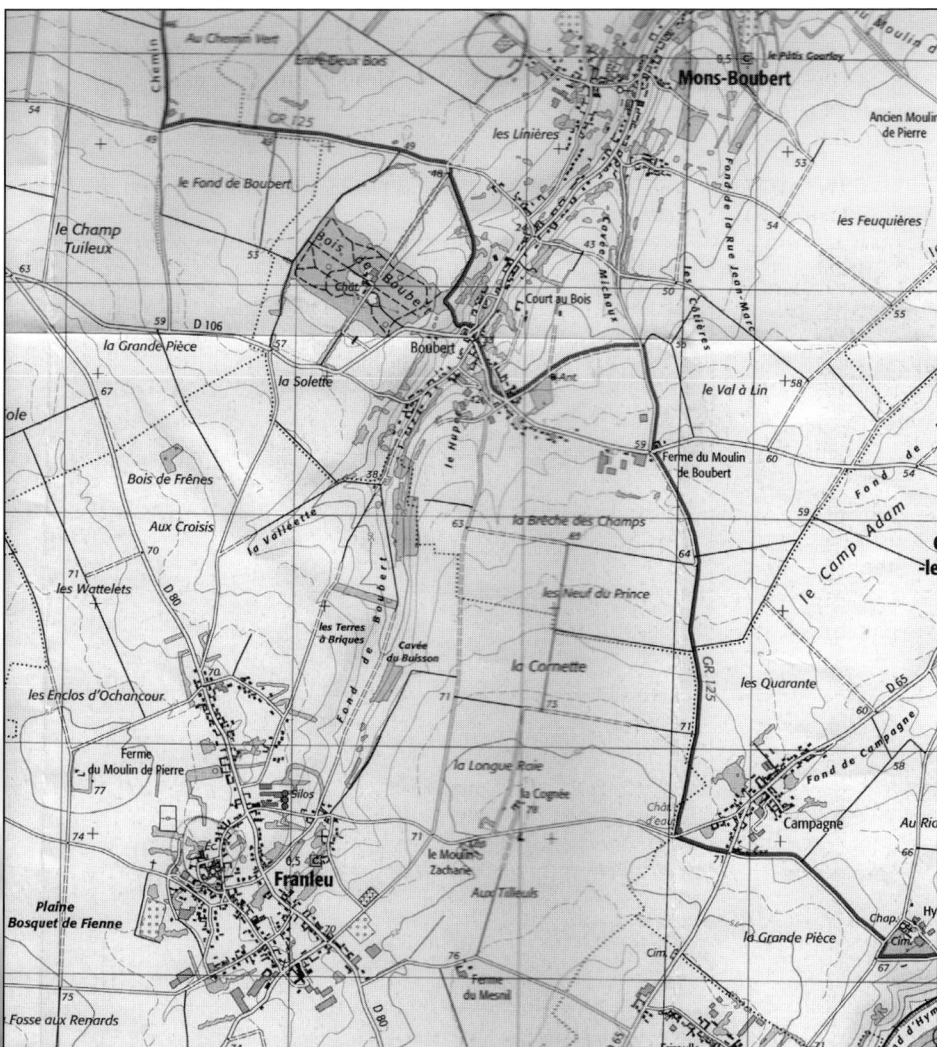

and back via the cemetery in Franleu. The walk may be split into two separate walks, Franleu and Mons-Boubert; or simply become a walk/drive. The choice is yours, but whatever you decide, bear in mind it is a little known battleground in two villages that still are much the same as they were in June 1940, and the inhabitants, although friendly, do not take it kindly to visitors tramping across their property.

Start: The Schoolhouse/Mairie at Franleu
Distance: 5.5 miles
Suitable for: 🚗 🚲 🚶
Finish: The churchyard cemetery at Franleu

The Mairie and schoolhouse are now in one and the same building. With the schoolhouse/Mairie on your left, head down **Rue des Écoles** until you reach Rue de L'Église. Turn left and proceed along to the D80. If you are walking, turn left for 0.07 miles and take **Rue de Boubert**, which will take you out of the village to **Boubert**. Those who elect to drive will need to take the next turning on the right, after the crossroads, towards the D106, where a right turn will take you to Boubert; at the intersection turn left. Turn along the D403 and continue for 0.7 miles until you see **Rue Delattre** on the left. Head along here for a further 0.35 miles and you will come to **Mons-Boubert Communal Cemetery**.

The cemetery at Mon-Boubert, where two men of the Highland Division rest.

At the far end of the cemetery are two graves, one belonging to Private Henderson and the other unnamed. Just what Henderson is doing in this cemetery remains a mystery but it is possible he died of wounds at Abbeville. The return journey is along **Rue Chouot Têtu L'y Branie**, which is almost opposite the local primary school, and at the end of the road turn right onto Rue Bas. This is the D403 which will take you to the D106. Turn right here and follow the road to retrace your steps back to **Franleu**. The **cemetery** is in the churchyard across the road and is a fitting way to end your excursion.

The Communal Cemetery at Franleu.

Walk 2: Huppy

Start: The monument on the D928
Distance: 2.36 miles
Suitable for: 🚗 🚲 🚶
Finish: The monument on the D928

The walk begins at the monument on the D928 where the D13 crosses the main road. The monument, written in French, commemorates the French victory of 28 May when de Gaulle took Huppy with the 4th Division Cuirassée from the Germans. De Gaulle appears to have a Huppy monopoly in that there are several plaques and monuments commemorating de Gaulle and none which refer to the British offensive involving the 2nd Armoured Brigade attack of 27 May. Nevertheless, it is part of the 1st Armoured Division's history and consequently worthy of inclusion.

The Huppy monument of the D928.

The heavy tank that was used by de Gaulle to capture Huppy.

Walk along **Route de Liercourt** and glance into the field to your left; this was the site of the 10/Royal Hussars tank attack of 27 May 1940. The left flank of the 2/Armoured Brigade crossed the road you are now standing on and **Schütze Hubert Brinkforth** of 14 Kompanie IR25 was in woods with his 3.7mm anti-tank gun on the left. (The woods have now disappeared.) His gun was responsible for wreaking havoc on eleven of the light tanks of the 10/Royal Hussars.

On McCreery's right flank the Queen's Bays were unaware of the 10/Hussars demise and pressed on towards Bailleul. Near the Bois de Limeux they ran into another German anti-tank position and four tanks were destroyed from the Bays' lead squadron. The attack was abandoned.

Continue along **Route de Liercourt** (D13) until you reach **Rue Baronne**, turn left along this road for 0.11 miles and then take a right turn along **Rue Dupré**, which will take you to Rue des Moulins. Continue along Rue des Moulins until you reach the Gothic fifteenth-century church of St Sulpice d'Huppy. Along the road, and fixed to the wall, are **two monuments to de Gaulle** and a signboard promoting the **Circuit de Mémoire de la Bataille d'Abbeville**. Return along Rue de l'Église ,which brings you to Route de Liercourt, turn right opposite the iron Gates and in 0.75 miles you will arrive back at your vehicle and the monument.

The Plaque commemorating the attack of May 29.

29 - 31 MAI 1940

LE GÉNÉRAL DE GAULLE
COMMANDAIT
LA 4ᵉ DIVISION CUIRASSÉE
AU COURS DES COMBATS
OÙ FUT BRISÉE
LA DÉFENSE ENNEMIE
DE HUPPY À MAREUIL-CAUBERT

SOUVENEZ VOUS
DU SACRIFICE DES SOLDATS
TOMBÉS POUR LA LIBERTÉ

REMEMBER

A larger memorial, incorporating a bust of de Gaulle.

Walk 3: St-Pierre-le-Viger and Houdetot

These two villages represent the last stand of the 1/Black Watch. At Ouville the Battalion received orders to take up positions on the railway line at St-Pierre-le-Viger, with the 5/Gordons on their left and possibly the French as well. From Ouville the road was packed with transport of all kinds, which was often stationary for some time. Eventually the companies got into position with B Company on the right, A Company in the centre and D Company on the left. C Company was in reserve and Battalion Headquarters in a small cottage near the sunken road. The French army was pouring over the crest of the hill and up the main road, which ran through the Black Watch lines. It was not an enviable position. The 5/Gordons were at the top of the hill, on the left of the road, probably along the line of the ridge.

At about 1.00pm orders were received to send a party to recce a new line running from Guetteville-les-Grès to Cailleville. Accordingly, D and C Company and all of HQ Company, less a section of carriers, were sent ahead, leaving A and B Companies and a skeleton force in Battalion

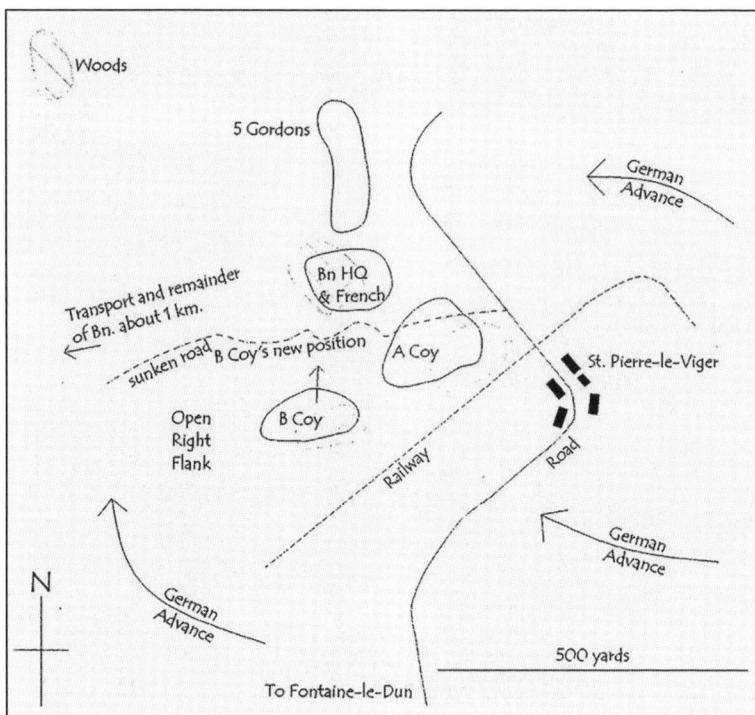

A map, originally drawn by Bradford, indicating the relative positions of the 1/Black Watch companies at St-Pierre-le-Viger.

146

A modern map of St-Pierre-le-Viger, showing details of the route to Houdetot.

Headquarters. At about 4.30 the Commanding Officer left for **Brigade Headquarters** and soon after the enemy began to engage them with mortar and machine gun fire. By 6.00pm they were heavily engaged and B Company withdrew to the shelter of the sunken road, but this only let the Germans advance very close to the Black Watch positions.

The position being held by the 1/Black Watch was as shown on the sketch made by **Captain Bradford** on 11 June 1940. At 8.00pm Bradford approached the French commander and spoke about the need for his men to retire. The French commander asked him to wait until dark. Shortly afterwards the Frenchman was badly wounded. At 9.00pm they decided to withdraw in conjunction with the French and made for the Guetteville-Cailleville Line, finally reaching Guetteville at about 1.30am on 12 June. Meanwhile, Lieutenant Colonel Honeyman had been prevented from returning along the sunken road by enemy vehicles and decided to brazen it out, finally surrendering on 13 June.

This route may be split into two sections, St-Pierre-le-Viger and Houdetot, although it should be said that the route is admirably suited to **bicycles**. Alternatively, it can be treated purely as a walk.

Start: St-Pierre-le-Viger, at the former station building
Distance: 4.3 miles
Suitable for: 🚗 🚲 🚶
Finish: St-Pierre-le-Viger

Find the railway line (now disused), which crosses the D142 by the former station building. A Company were in position just before the sunken road to Houdetot and B Company were in the station buildings. Battalion Headquarters and the French were across the sunken road in a cottage. The 5/Gordons were at the top of the hill, near to the wind turbines: their front line was the D142. B Company later moved to the shelter of the sunken road but, as we know, allowed the attacking Germans to close up on the 1/Black Watch positions.

At 9.00pm The Black Watch withdrew to Guetteville, leaving the remainder of the Battalion in **Houdetot**, where they expected them to rejoin the two companies that Bradford had commanded at St-Pierre-le-Viger. In fact Bradford left a guard on the crossroads at Guettevill in case the Battalion appeared

We are now going along the C3 minor road to find the remainder of the battalion. Head towards the sunken road and proceed along it until you catch a glimpse of the roofs of a private house on the right, Stop. This was the probable **site of the Battalion Headquarters**; it is certainly in the correct place, north of the sunken road.

Continue along the **C2 (Route d'Houdetot)** for about half a mile until you see a road junction, continue straight ahead until the next junction, go straight over and find Rue de la Motte du Castel. Go along here for 0.14

The start of the sunken road to Houdetot.

Is this the house that Bradford referred to as Battalion Headquarters?

The Churchyard Cemetery at Houdetot.

miles and turn left down Rue du Puits; at the end of this road turn left to find **Église St Pierre**.

This has a typical Normandy churchyard and the CWGC graves are to be found on either side of the church. There are seventeen men of the Highland Division buried here; but if Honeyman is correct in his estimation of deaths, then far more lie in unidentified graves or have been lost in communal burials. If you are walking or cycling, return along the same route back to St-Pierre-le-Viger.

Tour 1: Veules-les-Roses and St Valery-en-Caux

This tour is best completed in your vehicle as the distances involved and the geography make it almost impossible to walk or cycle with ease. The tour begins on the cliff tops above Veules-les-Roses on the D68 (Route de Veules).

Start: Parking du Canon
Distance: 10 miles
Suitable for: 🚗
Finish: The French monument

Parking du Canon is almost opposite the Les Mouettes campsite and can be reached by driving along the access road to the car park. A short walk across the field will bring you to the two guns that were salvaged from the wreck of the *Ceron*, which was targeted by German guns and subsequently destroyed. There are two information boards, in English and French, giving an account of the Battle of Vueles and have information about the ship itself. Another two plaques on a large stone gives the names of the French and British soldiers killed.

Over towards the town of Veules-les-Roses, on the left, at the edge of some scrubland, is a replica of a famous photograph depicting British soldiers as prisoners heading into captivity. (This is the same photograph that appears in Chapter 8, p. 117, and on the cover; and was published for the first time in the Nazi propaganda magazine *Signal*.)

The two salvaged guns of the *Ceron*, the central feature of the memorial.

Veules-les-Roses Communal Cemetery.

Our next stop is **Veules-les-Roses Communal Cemetery**, set on a slope on the west side of the town. Set your satnav for Rue Jean Maret and drive into the cemetery; the CWGC graves are at the far end of the cemetery. There are thirty-eight headstones, of which fourteen remain unidentified.

Back on the D925, stop at the **French Memorial**, which is between Ectot and Veules-les-Roses. The Memorial is opposite the wind turbines and was erected to commemorate the French 256th and 56th Regiment of Artillery between 1939–1945. It is likely that the ground it is built upon was purchased by the parents of Sous Lieutenant Pierre Thomas, one of five men who were killed here in 1940 and to whom the memorial is particularly dedicated.

At the roundabout on the D925 continue straight on and at the next roundabout take the D20, towards St Valery-en-Caux. This road will bring you the old station, which is now marked as a public place in the **Place de la Gare**. (A satnav is useful here.) The station building you can see was rebuilt after the war; during the war, and up until 1945, it remained one of the few buildings that were not damaged, The railway was inaugurated in July 1881 and opened between Motteville and St Valery-en-Caux, on a steep section from Vaast-Dieppedale.

On **17 January 1945**, nearly 2,000 American soldiers were travelling from Le Havre to fight on the Ardennes front when the train that was carrying

The French Memorial on the D925.

153

The railway station at St-Valery-en-Caux was rebuilt after the war.

them crashed into the station and demolished it. The entire train of forty-three wagons entered St Valery-en-Caux Station at about 80km per hour and over 350 soldiers were either killed or badly injured.

What were the Americans doing at St Valery-en-Caux? The American General Staff, in their wisdom, had decided to direct the Americans to the Lucky Strike rest camp at Janville, possibly as the ship bringing them to France had been torpedoed while still at sea. On 11 September 1994 a plaque commemorating the incident was fixed to the current station in a ceremony presided over by Sir Derek Lang. The station and railway line were closed in 1995.

Road names are frequently changed to commemorate particular actions. This one is on the D68 near Avenue Louis Savoye at St Valery-en-Caux.

This was also the place in 1940 that the 51st Division men were told to assemble prior to evacuation – except no-one was here to receive them. Major de Chimay, of the 1/Kensingtons, remembered being here and having no directions given to him. Chimay was quite specific that when they got to the station there was no sign of any guides and there were great numbers of troops milling around, crowded shoulder to shoulder. Take **Rue de la Grâce Dieu** and **Route du Havre** back to the town centre.

The **Tourist Information Centre** is to the left of the entrance to the Hotel de Ville (Mairie) on Quai d'Amont. We would recommend a stop here as a number of useful maps and street plans can be obtained free of charge. The famous photograph of **Rommel** standing next to General Fortune was taken outside the former Hotel de Ville building, which was rebuilt in the 1950s. The former sixteenth-century timber framed house, known as the house of Henri IV (Henri IV is said to have stayed there for one night in 1593) can clearly be seen on the photograph. The residence was built by Guillaume Ladiré in 1540 and today the house is home to a history museum, a memorial dedicated to the St Valery-en-Caux battle and an exhibition centre.

From the Hotel de Ville you will need to set your satnav to find **Avenue d'Escosse** and the **Franco-British Cemetery**. There are two entrances to this cemetery, one by the wooden gates at one end and the other, further up the road, by the entrance to the municipal cemetery, where there is parking. We used the municipal cemetery entrance, where a set of steps lead down to the Franco-British Cemetery. On entering the cemetery you will immediately notice that the Cross of Sacrifice marks the end of the British and the beginning of the French sections of the cemetery. This is a large cemetery

The famous photograph of Rommel standing with Victor Fortune.

The new Hotel de Ville, built on the site where Rommel stood with General Fortune.

The Franco-British Cemetery.

and contains many Highland Division men as well as a number of RAF and Commonwealth aircrew.

The **church on Rue d'Ectot**, a few yards down the road from the cemetery, was first built in the thirteenth century. A **stained glass window** depicting the entrance to the port and town was presented to the people of St Valery-en-Caux by the Highland cities and towns in Scotland to commemorate fifty years of solidarity. The window was created by Bradley Parker and the 51st (Highland) Division emblem can be seen at the very top of the window.

The stained glass window donated by the Highland cities and towns in Scotland to the people of St Valery-en-Caux.

From the church on Rue d'Ectot return to the Hotel de Ville and head to the east of the town, where a short trip up **Rue Raol Lessens** will eventually bring you to a car park. Or, if you are feeling energetic, there is a footpath from the Casino car park (signposted Monuments) leading uphill. However, from the car park it is a short walk to the Scottish and the Costes/Bellonte Monuments. The Dieudonné Costes and Maurice Bellonte monument commemorates the first successful flight between France and America in September 1930 in a Bregut Hispano. The **Memorial Scottish Stone** stands proudly on the east cliffs, commemorating the ill-fated attempt by the 51st (Highland) Division in June 1940 to defend France from German occupation. The inscription is engraved into the stone (see photograph). At the foot of the monument there are a number of stones commemorating various soldiers who were captured at Valery-en-Caux and a larger dedication to Trooper Sandy Ballie of the 1/Lothians, who was taken prisoner at St Valery-en-Caux and died in May 2005. The tour ends here or at the French Monument.

The French cliff monument can be clearly seen from the Scottish monument. This commemorates the men from the French divisions that were surrounded with the 51st Division by Rommel's 7th Panzer Division. The only way up to the French Monument is on foot, so be warned.

The memorial stone dedicated to the 51st Division.

The inscription on the stone.

51st (Highland) Division
Order of Battle

General Officer Commanding: Major General V.M. Fortune

152 Brigade: Brigadier H. Stewart (until 6 June, then Lt Col Barclay)
    2/Seaforths   4/Camerons
    4/Seaforths

153 Brigade: Brigadier G. Burney
    1/Gordons   4/Black Watch
    5/Gordons

154 Brigade: Brigadier A. Stanley-Clarke
    1/Black Watch   8/Argylls
    7/Argylls

Royal Artillery
    17/Field Regiment   75/Field Regiment
    23/Field Regiment   51/Anti-Tank Regiment

Royal Engineers
    26/Field Company,   238/Field Park Company
    236/Field Company,   213/Field Park Company
    237/Field Company,

Troops attached to the Division for the move to the Saar, April 1940

Royal Armoured Corps
    1/Lothians and Border Horse

Attached troops
Artillery
    1/RHA (less one battery)
    385 Battery, 97/Field Regiment
    51/Medium Regiment RA

Pioneers
    7/Royal Norfolk Regiment
    6/Royal Scots Fusiliers

Machine Gun Regiments
    1/Princess Louise's Kensington Regiment
    7/Royal Northumberland Fusiliers

From 7 June 1940
    'A' Brigade of the Beauman Division (late Beau Force)
    2/7 Duke of Wellington's Regiment

Bibliography

Ansell, Colonel Sir Michael, *Soldier On*, Peter Davis, 1973.

Barclay, Brigadier C.N., *The History of the Royal Northumberland Fusiliers in the Second World War*, William Clowes, 1952.

Blaxland, Gregory, *Destination Dunkirk*, Kimber, 1973.

Bradford, Andrew, *Escape from Saint Valery-en-Caux*, The History Press, 2009.

Barclay, Brigadier Cyril, *The History of the Royal Northumberland Fusiliers in the Second World War*, Clowes, 1952.

Cameron, Captain Ian, *History of the Argyll and Sutherland Highlanders 7th Battalion*, Nelson, 1947.

Committee of XRH Members, *The 10th Royal Hussars in The Second World War*, Gale & Polden, 1948.

David, Saul, *After Dunkirk*, Endeavour Ink, 2017.

Doherty, Richard, *None Bolder*, Spellmount, 2006.

Ellis, Major Lionel, *The War in France and Flanders*, Naval and Military Press, 2004.

Farndale, M., *History of the Royal Regiment of Artillery*, Brasseys, 1996.

Fergusson, Bernard, *The Black Watch – A Short History*, Woods, 1955.

Forczyk, Robert, *Case Red*, Osprey, 2017.

Gardener, Robert, *Kensington to St Valery-en-Caux*, Spellmount, 2002.

Innes, Bill (Editor), *St Valery. The Impossible Odds*, Birlinn, 2004.

Jackson, Julian, *The Fall of France*, OUP, 2003.

Karslake, Basil, *1940 The Last Act* , Leo Cooper, 1979.

Kemp, Colonel J.C., *The History of The Royal Scots Fusiliers*, GUP, 1963.

Liddel-Hart, Basil (Editor), *The Rommel Papers*, Collins, 1953.

Linklater, Eric, *The Highland Division*, HMST, 1942.

Lang, Derek, *Return to St Valery*, Leo Cooper, 1974.

Marshall-Cornwall, James, *Wars And Rumours of Wars*, Leo Cooper, 1984.

Murland, Jerry, *The Dunkirk Perimeter and Evacuation 1940*, Pen & Sword, 2019.

Shears, Phillip, *The Story Of The Border Regiment 1939–45*, Nisbet, 1948.

Whelan, Peter, *Useless Mouths*, Helion, 2018.

Williams, Douglas, *The New Contemptibles*, Murray, 1940.

Woods, Rex, *A Talent To Survive: The Wartime exploits of Richard Broad*, Kimber, 1982.

Contemporary Sources

Kensington Regiment War Diary, PRO WO 167/795, April to June 1940.

Kensington Regiment War Diary, PRO WO 166/4350, July to September 1940.

Index

Dear Reader,

We hope you have enjoyed this book, but why not share your views on social media? You can also follow our pages to see more about our other products: facebook.com/penandswordbooks or follow us on Twitter @penswordbooks

You can also view our products at www.pen-and-sword.co.uk (UK and ROW) or www.penandswordbooks.com (North America).

To keep up to date with our latest releases and online catalogues, please sign up to our newsletter at: www.pen-and-sword.co.uk/newsletter

If you would like a printed catalogue with our latest books, then please email: enquiries@pen-and-sword.co.uk or telephone: 01226 734555 (UK and ROW) or email: Uspen-and-sword@casematepublishers.com or telephone: (610) 853-9131 (North America).

We respect your privacy and we will only use personal information to send you information about our products.

Thank you!